VGM Professional Careers Series

CAREERS
IN MARKETING

LILA B. STAIR
LESLIE STAIR

THIRD EDITION

VGM Career Books

Chicago   New York   San Francisco   Lisbon   London   Madrid   Mexico City
Milan   New Delhi   San Juan   Seoul   Singapore   Sydney   Toronto

Library of Congress Cataloging-in-Publication Data

Stair, Lila B.
    Careers in marketing / Lila B. Stair and Leslie Stair. — 3rd ed..
      p.   cm. — (VGM professional careers series)
    ISBN 0-658-02116-8 (hardcover) — ISBN 0-658-02117-6 (pbk.)
    1. Marketing—Vocational guidance.   I. Stair, Leslie.   II. Title.   III. Series.

HF5415.122 .S72   2001
658.8'0023'73—dc21   2001026426

VGM Career Books

A Division of The McGraw·Hill Companies

1 2 3 4 5 6 7 8 9 0   LBM/LBM   0 9 8 7 6 5 4 3 2 1

ISBN 0-658-02116-8 (hardcover)
ISBN 0-658-02117-6 (paperback)

This book was set in Times
Printed and bound by Lake Book Manufacturing

Cover photograph copyright © PhotoDisc

McGraw-Hill books are available at special quantity discounts to use as premiums and sales promotions, or for use in corporate training programs. For more information, please write to the Director of Special Sales, Professional Publishing, McGraw-Hill, Two Penn Plaza, New York, NY 10121-2298. Or contact your local bookstore.

This book is printed on acid-free paper.

To Terri, our favorite plethora of knowledge

To Tony, Ryan, John, and Grant for making this
wonderful internship experience possible

CONTENTS

in public relations. Sources of public relations information. The importance of customer service in today's economy. Customer service sales. Technology and customer service.

ABOUT THE AUTHORS

Lila Stair is a professional author in the areas of careers and business. She holds an M.A. in counseling from the University of New Orleans and an M.B.A. from Florida State University. As an instructor of business courses at both community college and university levels, she has had the opportunity both to teach business concepts and to assist students in selecting business careers. Formerly a career counselor, Lila Stair has worked with hundreds of students. In addition to counseling and providing students with career information, she has also worked with employers in job development and placement. To assist individuals in researching and making career choices, she has developed a model for evaluating careers in terms of aptitudes, interests, and values, which appears in the preface of this book.

Leslie Stair has studied business and communications at Tulane University in New Orleans and has served as secretary of the Alpha Kappa Psi business fraternity. Working on the professional committee for the fraternity, she arranged speakers for the group, learning from these professionals the importance of such areas as internships, networking, resume development, and interviewing skills. An internship at the Charles W. Schwab branch in Tallahassee, Florida, allowed her to experience the power of computers and information firsthand in marketing financial services.

PREFACE

Choosing a college major that leads to a satisfying career is not easy. The choices are many and varied. Often students opt for college majors based on academic aptitudes, a single strong interest, personal values, or market factors which sometimes change. Experiencing the work itself as early as possible through part-time jobs and internships will help individuals realize whether or not they have chosen wisely from the millions of jobs available. The field of marketing offers many opportunities. According to the U.S. Bureau of Labor Statistics, marketing and sales jobs will grow by 2.3 million from 1998 to 2008, with a large number of these in services industries. Advertising, marketing, and public relations managers, management analysts, and college and university professors are among the fastest growing occupations.

Marketing professionals are employed in every type of industry and nonprofit organization, including government. Employment with large advertising, sales promotion, public relations, and consulting agencies offers the possibility of advancement to partner, enabling an individual to share proportionately in the profits of the agency. Marketing fields also offer numerous options for self-employment as manufacturers' agents, entrepreneurs, and consultants in such areas as marketing strategy, public relations, and advertising. Whatever an individual's interests and values, marketing has something to offer.

Career decision-making is complex because it requires a careful analysis of one's strengths and weaknesses and it has a major impact on one's quality of life and the achievement of personal goals. A career decision-making model that incorporates both internal and external factors affecting career choice follows. The blank lines in the model enable career decision makers to add factors important to them and to rank the factors in terms of their relative importance. It was developed to enable individuals to better evaluate the career options discussed in this book.

Career Decision- Making Model

Internal factors	External factors
Aptitudes and attributes	**Family influence**
_____ Academic aptitudes and achievement	_____ Family values and expectations
_____ Occupational aptitudes and skills	_____ Socioeconomic level
_____ Social skills	_____ _____
_____ Communication skills	_____ _____
_____ Leadership abilities	_____ _____
_____ _____	_____ _____
_____ _____	_____ _____
_____ _____	_____ _____
Interests	**Economic influence**
_____ Amount of supervision	_____ Overall economic conditions
_____ Amount of pressure	_____ Employment trends
_____ Amount of variety	_____ Job market information
_____ Amount of work with data	_____ _____
_____ Amount of work with people	_____ _____
_____ _____	_____ _____
_____ _____	_____ _____
_____ _____	_____ _____
_____ _____	_____ _____
Values	**Societal influence**
_____ Salary	_____ Perceived effect of race, sex, or
_____ Status/prestige	ethnic background on success
_____ Advancement opportunity	_____ Perceived effect of physical or
_____ Growth on the job	psychological handicaps on success
_____ _____	_____ _____
_____ _____	_____ _____
_____ _____	_____ _____
_____ _____	_____ _____
_____ _____	_____ _____

Among the factors influencing an individual's career choice are careers of family members, guidance from teachers, suggestions from friends, personal interests, and values. A college education requires a large commitment of time, money, and energy, and selecting a college major demands careful consideration. Even students who have already chosen a college major should explore other options early in their education to be sure that they have chosen wisely. Some students become dissatisfied with their original choice when they begin to take courses in the field and end up wanting to change majors. Advisors assigned to students can provide some help, but most are not career specialists.

Today, most college campuses have career information centers available both to students and members of the community who are interested in exploring career options. User-friendly computerized career information systems are available in many college career centers. These systems aid students in making career choices by relating responses on a questionnaire to various careers and generating a list of career options based on the responses. Students can then obtain descriptions of careers that look interesting. Many computerized systems provide information on colleges and financial aid as well. Career centers house a plethora of printed career information, including occupational briefs, current articles, and books such as *Careers in Marketing*.

It is our hope that all who explore marketing careers through this book will gain the insights and enthusiasm for marketing that we have gained in writing it. In addition to job descriptions, this book includes personal and educational requirements for those entering marketing careers, salary data, job market information, trends, job search tips, and many sources of additional information. Challenges and rewards abound for those entering the field of marketing. The first and greatest challenge is to prepare and market oneself. It is the objective of this book to help in this end.

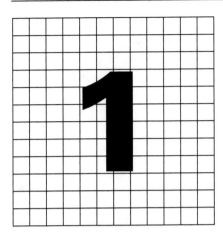

MARKETING IN THE NEW MILLENNIUM

Marketers in the twenty-first century had better know their browsers, cookies, and ISPs. The computer plays a significant role in every aspect of our lives, impacting the way we live, play, and learn. E-commerce is affecting how we become aware of new products, what products we eventually buy, and the manner in which we purchase them. The Internet economy is growing very rapidly and is giving birth to new companies offering a wide variety of products online. Many online resources offer marketing professionals information on consumers and ways to improve every aspect of the marketing process. A conservative estimate is that the number of Americans using the Internet increases by 4 percent every three months. Another survey claims that every second, seven new people around the globe tap into the Internet for the first time.[1] An incredible number of websites have been developed to offer these Internet users information and products in every conceivable area including health, travel, job placement, and investment. It is not surprising that the Internet economy now plays an important part in marketing careers.

Demographics significantly impact the types of products offered and the number of available workers. By 2006 the number of people between the prime working ages of 25 and 44 will have declined nearly 12 percent, while those aged 45 to 64 who are positioning themselves for retirement will have increased substantially. People are continuing to live longer with a growing number of those aged 65 and over. Many in this group will still be caring for elderly parents and may have to work longer. Having children later in life will affect the level of affluence in many families, and people will therefore be able to afford more consumer products for their children. Marketers must take into consideration everything that impacts what products they produce and the number of qualified workers available to produce those products.

No field in business offers a greater variety of career choices than marketing. Challenges in the field abound, as marketers grapple with new technology, demographics, an economy in flux, changing tastes and values, emerging and disappearing brands, and numerous other factors that affect marketing decisions. Consumers are bombarded with information about product offerings from thousands of companies of all sizes. These companies offer far more than just products, however, as they also offer many excellent career opportunities.

THE EVOLUTION OF THE FIELD OF MARKETING

Marketing is by no means a new field. In fact, it has been around since primitive tribes began to barter or exchange goods that were plentiful for those that were scarce. They traded grain, meat, jewelry, hides, and other items. The notion of trade existed in prehistoric times and was not so different from what it is today. The board of directors of the American Marketing Association defines marketing as "the process of planning and executing the conception, pricing, promotion, and distribution of ideas, goods, and services to create exchanges that satisfy individual and organizational objectives." The notion of a product has been expanded to include ideas and services as well as goods. As the definition suggests, marketing professionals are involved in every stage of the formation of a product—from its conception to its actual sale and distribution.

The field of marketing has evolved over the centuries. The early American settlers were farmers, producing what they needed to survive. By trading with other settlers and Native Americans, they were part of the *production era* of marketing that lasted roughly 300 years. During these years, production evolved into a custom process that provided consumers with goods of value for which they would exchange other goods, gold, or money. Initially, products were produced only on customer demand. By the 1800s, however, producers were beginning to anticipate consumer demand and were creating products ahead of time.

The Industrial Revolution developed and was in full swing by the second half of the nineteenth century, and the mass production of consumer products began. Unlike the early part of the century, when small quantities were produced and customers were geographically close to producers, mass production created the need for sales and distribution strategies.

Thus, marketing entered its *sales era* at the beginning of the twentieth century. Producers began to have more products to sell than they had customers, so they turned their attention to sales techniques. The hard sell was born and used to the extent that consumerism allowed. Most people think of consumerism as a fairly recent phenomenon, but it actually began in the early 1900s. Legislation regulating both product quality and misleading advertising was enacted prior to World War II. However, with consumer products scarce during the war, people were happy to get what they could. But by the 1950s, the economy was booming and products were again plentiful. It was at this time that the *marketing era* began.

The marketing era is characterized by a shift from the previous sales orientation to a market orientation. Today, the primary emphasis is no longer on selling already planned and produced goods, but rather identifying customer wants and planning products to satisfy these wants. The *marketing concept* is a philosophy that focuses on customer wants and identified markets. Companies have found that they can create the desire for certain types of products in well-defined groups of potential customers. Thus, marketing has grown into a complex and sophisticated field needing a large number of highly trained professionals to perform its many specialized functions.

THE SCOPE OF THE MARKETING FIELD

The dramatic evolution of the marketing era increased marketing's functions from advertising and selling, which dominated the sales era, to include marketing research, product development, packaging, promotion, and public relations. Marketing begins with the identification of the need for a product, which can be a good or a service, by a particular market. Marketing research specialists perform this job. Marketing researchers locate potential consumer groups, describe them in detail, find out what these consumers want, consider these wants in terms of specific products, determine if such products exist and which competing companies are supplying them, forecast what products consumers are likely to buy in the future, and which competitors are likely to produce them. And that's only part of it!

Once a product is conceived, the idea is turned over to product development. Professionals under the direction of a product manager then plan the product in detail. This planning doesn't end with the product itself but includes its price, packaging, and distribution. Product management is also involved in all other marketing functions. Additional information may be required from marketing research throughout the planning phase, and ideas for promoting the product may come directly from the product specialists.

There are three major ways to promote a product: advertising, personal selling, and sales promotion. Advertising is a nonpersonal presentation using a variety of media such as television, radio, newspapers, magazines, handbills, billboards, and the Internet. Personal selling involves direct customer contact. Sales promotion, a concept born of the marketing era, involves three types of product promotion: consumer promotion, trade promotion, and sales force promotion.

Public relations (PR) is a completely separate function from advertising and sales promotion. Public relations specialists work to project a positive company image and to create goodwill with the public. Consumerism is alive and well in today's economy. Consumer watchdog groups regularly publicize business practices with which they don't agree. For instance, the tuna company that kills dolphins earns the ill will of both environmentalists and others who love dolphins. Environmentalists who have taken on the responsibility of monitoring the effects of both products and production processes on the environment and publicizing the results use public relations very effectively. Manufacturers must, in turn, mount public relations campaigns to counter charges and maintain a positive image. Green marketing has been a strategy for many years. Rising interest in eco-friendly cars has caused manufacturers both in Detroit and Japan to begin the introduction of cars with fuel-efficient, gasoline-electric power trains into the market.[2]

Cause marketing has become even more popular with the advent of the Internet. For example, Pura Vida Coffee (www.puravidacoffee.com), created in 1999 by John Sage, a retired Microsoft executive, and Chris Dearnley, a pastor in Costa Rica, donates 100 percent of net profits to a locally run ministry and to social programs that help the poorest children and families in Costa Rica.[3] Yahoo! Auctions, one of the largest, globally branded free auction sites on the Internet, auctioned off autographed jeans donated by over seventy celebrities with proceeds going to the National Multiple Sclerosis Society's Southern California Chapter.[4] HardCloud.com sponsored "Boarding for Breast Cancer," a charity snowboarding event to raise money for organizations such as The Susan G. Komen Foundation, The Nina Hyde Center for Breast Cancer Research, and numerous local organizations.[5] In 1999 the U.S. Surgeon General hosted the African American Community HIV/AIDS Satellite Conference, which was broadcast over the BlackFamilies.com website to educate and mobilize the community to fight against the disease.[6] These causes are promoted and marketed like any other product and offer marketers opportunities to do worthwhile and satisfying work.

Nonprofit organizations such as charities, the arts, educational institutions, and federal and local governments use the marketing concept to promote their causes as well. When a nonprofit organization is soliciting funds or promoting ideas, it functions in much the same way as a business selling goods or services. The expanded scope of marketing in society today accounts for the many jobs available to those with marketing backgrounds.

AN OVERVIEW OF MARKETING CAREERS

An understanding of the variety and quantity of different careers in marketing can be gleaned from the breadth of the marketing function itself. Figure 1.1 shows key management positions and functional areas in the field of marketing and how they relate to one another. Corporate marketing management positions are discussed in Chapter 8.

Marketing Research

Approaching the functional areas chronologically in terms of the marketing process, the first major area is marketing research. Manufacturers must learn whether consumers will buy a proposed product before committing huge amounts of time and money to developing and introducing it. This is the work of marketing research professionals. The marketing research department of a company includes the director of marketing research, researcher analysts, and trainees. These individuals generally have degrees in marketing with strong backgrounds in statistics and psychology. Researcher analysts may also work in marketing research firms or as independent consultants. The field of mar-

Figure 1.1 Management of Marketing Functions

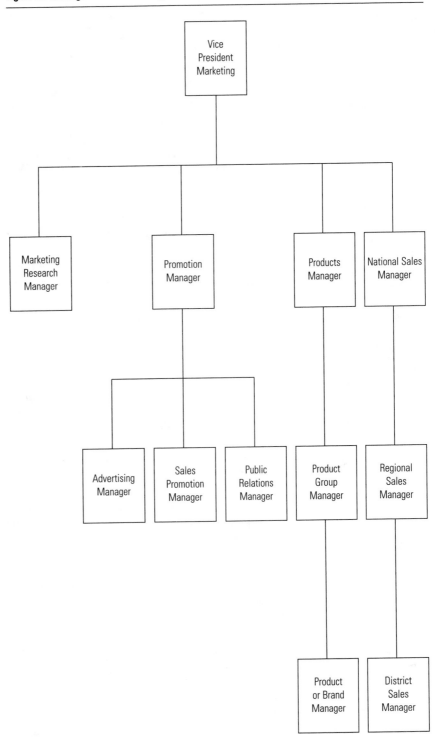

keting research will be explored in Chapter 2 along with the specific duties of these professionals.

Product Development

Once an industrial firm makes a commitment to developing a specific product, a product manager is assigned or hired to spearhead the project. This position is often entitled "brand manager" in firms producing consumer products. The manager assembles a development team whose members work first with marketing researchers to further define the characteristics of the product, then with engineers in the design and production phases of product development, with advertising and sales promotion professionals, and finally with sales personnel. Members of the product development team are involved in naming, packaging, and distributing the product. They usually come from different departments throughout the organization. As team members, they are in a unique position to interact with almost every department in the company. Product development can be an excellent avenue of advancement to other positions within the company because it is very visible. Chapter 3 details the work of the development team from the inception to the completion of the project.

Advertising

Of all marketing careers, advertising is perhaps the most competitive. Whether employed by a company or an advertising agency, professionals must work in a highly charged atmosphere with extreme pressure to produce. In a company, the advertising manager determines how to spend the advertising budget and creative personnel design and produce the advertisements. These ads are then turned over to media professionals who plan marketing strategy and buy airtime on television or radio and space in printed media or on the Internet. Research professionals study both consumers' perceptions of products and advertising effectiveness. They also interact with creative and media personnel in the initial production of ads and in subsequent modifications of ad campaigns. The advertising manager must decide for each product whether to conduct the ad campaign completely in-house or whether to hire an outside advertising agency. Advertising professionals employed by agencies perform the same functions as described above. Normally advertising agencies have four departments: creative, media, research, and account services. In the account services department an account executive oversees the ad campaign and serves as the liaison between the agency and the client. Chapter 4 describes an especially wide range of advertising positions with varying backgrounds and duties.

Sales Promotion

In addition to advertising, sales promotion and public relations campaigns generate sales. These two areas are completely separate and have totally different objectives. Closely linked to advertising, which is a nonpersonal presentation, sales promotion targets individual consumers. Advertising suggests while sales promotion motivates. Sales promotion falls into three categories: (1) consumer promotion, including samples, coupons, rebates, games, contests, and other incentives; (2) trade promotion for intermediaries, including cooperative ads, free goods, and dealer sales contests; and (3) sales force promotion, including such incentives as sales meetings, contests for prizes, and bonuses. Specialists in sales promotion usually have previous sales or advertising experience. These professionals may be employed by producer companies or sales promotion agencies, which play a role similar to advertising agencies as discussed in Chapter 4.

Public Relations

Both sales promotion and advertising focus on specific products. The sale of all products in a company may be improved through the creation of goodwill. The mission of a public relations department is to build and maintain the company's positive image. Large companies have public relations departments with staffs of specialists who work under a director of public relations. Smaller companies may hire one individual to conduct public relations activities. Some organizations hire public relations agencies that function in the same manner as advertising or sales promotion agencies. Public relations specialists provide information about the organization to news media, arrange speaking engagements for company officials, and usually write the speeches for these engagements. Individuals need not have marketing degrees to enter public relations; in fact, public relations people tend to come from an incredibly wide variety of backgrounds. However, they are all involved in selling—selling the organization to the public. Public relations easily fits into the marketing effort of a company, as can be seen in Chapter 5.

Distribution and Sales

The combined efforts of advertising, sales promotion, and public relations professionals create consumer awareness of a company and its products. The producer must then choose how to transport its products from warehouses to the consumers. This process, called distribution, may be done through various channels. Options include the sale of the product to wholesalers, retailers, or directly to the consumer.

Sales and customer service are the keys to running a successful business in today's economy. Professional salespeople are the backbone of any company. Without an effective sales force, a company could not survive in a competitive, global environment. With so many similar products, it is the sales force that makes the difference. Many marketing graduates start in sales. This area is where beginners truly learn their company's business and make contributions to profits. It is an opportunity for an individual's hard work to really pay off both in increased earnings and in recognition.

Retail salespeople sell products to the final consumer. Wholesale and industrial sales personnel sell both finished products and basic materials to retailers, other intermediate agents, and manufacturers. Industrial sales representatives are employed by manufacturers, but they are not the only ones selling the company's products. Manufacturers' representatives are independent businesspeople who may sell one or more companies' products to many different customers. Finally, self-employed wholesale dealers find needed products for client companies. Chapters 6 and 7 describe wholesaling and retailing.

Direct marketing, or nonstore selling, is growing at a faster rate than in-store selling and includes such methods as direct selling, direct response retailing, database marketing, direct mail, and teleservices. E-commerce is another method of selling directly to the consumer. Direct marketing offers a variety of career opportunities and will be discussed in Chapter 6.

Marketing careers are varied and interesting. Depending on a person's verbal or quantitative strengths, interests, creativity, sales flair, and initiative, one of these careers could be a wise choice and provide opportunities for success. After gaining more in-depth information on all of these careers, individuals will be better able to choose a specific area within the field of marketing that is compatible with both their interests and aptitudes.

TRENDS AFFECTING MARKETING CAREERS

Marketing occurs in an ever-changing environment to which marketing professionals must adapt. The economy of the 1990s was bolstered by a number of knowledge-driven industries including computer hardware, computer software, telecommunications, the Internet, film and TV production, financial services, medical research, and tourism. According to some estimates, the economy has a long-term growth potential of between 2 and 2.5 percent a year. To maintain a noninflationary growth rate, the Federal Reserve Board adjusts short-term interest rates and keeps a close eye on prices. Positive economic signs include a surge in productivity, an increase in highly skilled workers, efficient capital investment, expanding global trade, more affordable and useful information technologies, an increase in patent applications, and a rapidly growing Internet economy. Productivity in both manufacturing and service sectors is on the rise, and many of the new graduates entering the job market must be prepared to enter the service sector.

Marketers in the 1990s operated in a highly price-conscious environment in which customers had increasingly greater and more convenient access to information. This is also the case in the 2000s when millions of consumers have access to a plethora of price and product information via the Internet. The preponderance of online businesses in recent years has raised questions about the lack of Internet sales tax and privacy issues related to marketing methods. Local and state governments are considering the taxation issue, while the federal government passed digital-signature legislation in June 1999, giving legal backing to online signatures.[7] In this new environment of online and offline competition, customers should be viewed as assets and customer service is tantamount to retaining those assets. The marketing of both goods and services will focus on value to the customer as well as customer service, which will be discussed in detail in Chapter 5.

The markets of the 1970s changed dramatically with the introduction of new technologies, the flood of imports, and the deregulation of airlines and other industries. The 1980s became a decade of mergers and acquisitions as organizations attempted to remain profitable or grow through restructuring. This upheaval created opportunities for entrepreneurs who found market niches or small groups of consumers with unfilled needs for specific goods or services. Record numbers of new small businesses were created to meet these needs. Throughout the 1980s and 1990s, an entrepreneurial boom occurred. Though the number of new small businesses is decreasing in this decade, small business owners still provide many new jobs in the economy, particularly E-businesses that grow more rapidly than traditional small businesses. Chapter 10 describes opportunities for entrepreneurs, franchisees, educators, and consultants.

During the 1990s the economy experienced major changes. The North American Free Trade Agreement (NAFTA) and the General Agreement on Tariffs and Trade (GATT) removed many trade barriers in North America, Europe, and Asia and facilitated economic globalization. Improvements in network information technology and their impact on our knowledge-based economy have enabled businesses to compete in the global economy. E-Latin Business (elb.com) provides technological and financial support and guidance to Internet companies wanting to do business in Latin America.[8] Opportunities in global marketing will continue to increase as technology makes foreign markets more accessible, and as American business moves abroad, the need for individuals who are familiar with foreign languages and cultures will grow substantially. Those who are prepared to assume a role in global marketing will find excellent career possibilities, which will be discussed in Chapter 9.

Another trend that affects the field of marketing is the increase in minority populations. The Hispanic American population is the fastest growing minority group in the U.S. today. Companies such as Heineken have created marketing campaigns for Hispanic audiences featuring television commercials that reflect Hispanic values and radio spots using Hispanic actors.[9] Changing lifestyles and values also have a dramatic impact on markets and products. Working women, who control more and more of the wealth, help to contribute to the success of shops that offer the convenience of quick shopping with no lines. Additionally, our more health-conscious public is demanding lower fat content in foods, and because of this, new fat-free products appear daily on grocery shelves.

A CAREER IN MARKETING

An investigation of careers in marketing reveals a variety of challenging professions, including high-interest fields such as advertising and less known fields such as marketing research. Marketing attracts large numbers of people with a wide range of interests, experiences, and educational backgrounds. Of all majors open to college business and communications majors, marketing offers the widest range of career choices. Marketing managers at all levels hold positions with considerable power because the marketing of products directly affects how companies generate revenues. In a recent study of business students in the United States, the Philippines, and New Zealand, most students chose marketing management as their preferred career path, followed by management consulting, public relations, product management, and international sales.[10]

Interest inventories can help students make more informed career decisions. James Waldroop and Timothy Butler, the directors of MBA career-development programs at the Harvard Business School, conducted a twelve-year study of Harvard business students and developed the Business Career Interest Inventory (BCII), which identified eight core sets of activities and related them to successful businesspeople. For example, individuals such as advertising executives, brand managers, salespeople, and public relations specialists are interested in both "creative production," involving highly creative activities, and "influence through language and ideas," involving the use of persuasion to exercise influence over others. Successful CEOs and marketing managers may share interests in both "enterprise control," which involves having strategy and decision-making authority and resource control over an operation, and "influence through language and ideas." For entrepreneurs, short-term project managers, new-product developers, and advertising "creatives," the activity that dominates their interest is "creative production."[11]

Marketing jobs offer creativity, challenge, and variety. Today, marketing places a greater emphasis on both customer satisfaction and on how to best provide services in our service-oriented economy. An investigation of careers in marketing will point out specific areas of opportunity and the broad nature of marketing as a whole. Successful career preparation requires mastering knowledge and skills in a discipline and educating oneself to compete in today's job market. Our exploration of marketing careers begins at the start of the marketing process: marketing research.

1. Harvey, Mary. "Elements of E-commerce Success." *Folio Special Source Book Issue* (2000): 192–194.
2. Buss, Dale. "Green Cars." *American Demographics*, January 2001, 58.
3. "Online Coffee Company Devotes 100% of Profits to Help Kids in Need." *Business Wire*, April 19, 1999.
4. "Celebrity 'Jean Therapy' Raises Funds and Awareness for National Multiple Sclerosis Society Through Yahoo! Auctions." *Canada News Wire*, April 28, 2000.
5. "HardCloud Helps Raise Awareness for Breast Cancer." *PR Newswire*, April 5, 2000.
6. "World Wide Web, Government and Community Organizations Unite to Address Rising AIDS Epidemic in African-American Community with Unprecedented Satellite Conference." *PR Newswire*, November 23, 1999.
7. Anders, Jason. "Net Capitol." *The Wall Street Journal*, July 17, 2000, R10.
8. "Hispanic Marketing Executive and Fortune 500 Brand Manager Manuel G. Gonzalez Joins ELB Group as President." *PR Newswire*, May 8, 2000.
9. "Heineken Launches Integrated Marketing Effort Targeted at Hispanic America." *Business Wire*, April 12, 1999.
10. Honeycutt, Earl D., Jr., et al. "Student Preferences for Sales Careers Around the Pacific Rim." *Industrial Marketing Management* 28 (January 1999).
11. Waldroop, James, and Timothy Butler. "Finding the Job You Should Want." *Fortune*, March 2, 1998, 211–214.

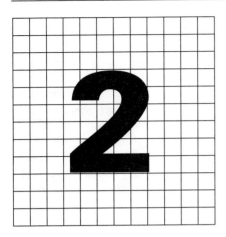

CAREERS IN MARKETING RESEARCH

Marketing research as a field has existed for about fifty years. Over this time it has continued to evolve and change. Today, access to valuable information via the Internet has substantially impacted marketing research, enabling researchers to share information more easily. The definition of *marketing research* as defined in 1991 by the American Marketing Association is "the use of scientific methods to identify and define marketing opportunities and problems, generate, refine, and evaluate marketing actions, monitor marketing performance, and improve our understanding of marketing as a process."[1] Identifying current fads and future trends, as well as what consumers are buying now and what they will buy in the future—this is the challenge facing marketing researchers. Predicting what consumers will buy in the future is tricky business, and mistakes can be very costly to companies. The scientific approach of marketing research provides a means to help minimize new product failures.

Marketing researchers must constantly monitor market performance, consumer knowledge, attitudes, values, needs, demographics, and all components in society that affect what goods and services are offered to the public. Marketing research is important in today's society because it is an important means for determining such offerings. Businesses today must respond to changes in consumer attitude and demographics in order to stay competitive. A recent study of marketing research executives identified significant changes in consumers' attitudes and demographics, including a perceived loss of privacy and lack of trust in business and government; aging and wellness with active baby boomers; increased life expectancy; a growing impact of teen consumers; and an increase in diversity. These changes have greatly increased the number of focus groups marketers must target.[2]

Technology is creating many new possibilities for marketing researchers. The Internet provides the opportunity for accessing timely information and having real-time dialogs with consumers. Rapid transportation and high-speed communications grant speedy access to products and services as well as information. With U.S. exports reaching almost $1 trillion in 1999, according to the U.S. Bureaus of Census and Economic Analysis, globalization creates both the opportunity and the need for research that analyzes differences in cultures, tastes, and business practices.

In order to grow, companies must use their resources to increase the sales of existing products or introduce new ones. One of the most important decisions facing marketing managers is whether or not to develop a new product. Successful new products can potentially generate huge profits for a company. However, products that fail can be a company's undoing. Because of the cost of developing and launching a new product in today's competitive market, most companies cannot afford too many failures—but nonetheless, they do occur. Sometimes products that we like suddenly disappear from the shelves. Good products that are ineffectively marketed can be as unprofitable as inferior products that should never have been produced. While success depends on the entire marketing process working as it should, it all begins with marketing research.

THE MARKETING RESEARCH PROCESS

New technology and techniques provide the accurate and timely information vital to the marketing research process. A systems approach to marketing information made possible by advances in computer technology enables orderly collection, analysis, and dissemination of the information managers need to make decisions. Managers specify the kind, amount, and quality of information that they require and turn these specifications over to their marketing research departments. Marketing research is the process of identifying and defining an opportunity, such as a target market or an unfilled need, collecting and analyzing the data relevant to this opportunity, and presenting the information to marketing managers. Although some ideas for products originate in marketing research, an idea can come from any source, including a company's competitors.

In the past, Japan has proven the adage that "imitation is the purest form of flattery" by improving on already-developed products and capturing the largest share of the market. Today however, the Japanese have moved to the forefront of high technology through sophisticated intelligence work. Japanese marketing researchers collect information on every aspect of American culture and technology, especially in research labs of American universities where ideas are germinated.

The marketing research department must not only have a clear idea of the current state of the company's customers, potential customers, and competitors, but it must also be looking forward. Analysts must carefully monitor changing tastes and lifestyles in order to predict what people will want in the future. The growing teen market is influencing both products being introduced and the manner in which they are marketed. Called the most global market of all, teens around the world have surprisingly similar tastes and attitudes. Adult sensibility, bizarre fashion combinations, and a passion for the newest technologies are traits that characterize teenagers today. Teens are only one of many groups served by the economy. Other larger groups include women, Hispanics, and

African Americans. In the past, marketers have targeted these groups. Today's economy has further diversified into dozens of specific subgroups defined by age, lifestyle, neighborhood, and combinations of such characteristics. It is up to marketing researchers to define these numerous market segments and predict future buying trends.

Ideas for new products come from trends identified through marketing research. Depending on the product, development can take a very long time. For example, years of development and testing are required from the time an automobile design leaves the drawing board and the finished product hits the showroom floor. Many products are rendered obsolete during the development cycle by competitors' products or technological innovations.

THE WORK OF MARKETING RESEARCHERS

Marketing research professionals engage in a long list of research activities such as:

Monitoring competitors

Identifying market trends

Developing customer profiles

Measuring market share

Evaluating brand images

Designing products and packages

Planning distribution channels

Assisting in advertising and promotion campaigns

Analyzing audience characteristics

Evaluating the impact of advertising and promotion

These research activities involve collecting data from a variety of sources. Primary data are collected through original research for a specific purpose, and the process is usually very costly. Primary data can come from company personnel, actual and potential customers, or even competitors (usually without their cooperation). These data are normally obtained through observation, experimentation, or survey. Consumer behavior may be observed and recorded in stores. Experimentation may include taste tests. Measuring the effect of advertising, price changes, and product or packaging alterations on consumer buying practices is a type of experimentation. Researchers conduct surveys by mail, telephone, or in person to get consumer reactions to existing or proposed products. Secondary data have been previously collected by individuals inside or outside the firm and may be part of company records or large databases. Since secondary data are usually cheaper and faster to acquire than primary data, researchers normally begin the research process by collecting and analyzing all relevant secondary data.

Marketing research provides management with the information needed to develop a marketing strategy, including potential market share, sales, price, promotion, and channels of distribution. When companies decide to develop new products, designers develop prototypes on the basis of marketing research and the prototypes are then tested for marketability. Marketing research professionals oversee market testing, report results, and make recommendations. Options include abandoning development, altering the product in some way, or planning the promotion strategy. Marketing researchers are part of product development teams and contribute vital information to the entire product development process. Product development will be discussed in detail in Chapter 3.

The scope of marketing research is not limited to consumer products. Research may be conducted in such areas as environmental concerns, business decisions, political campaigns, association images, and a wide range of others. Regardless of the particular research question or problem, all research involves data collection and analysis. It may be quantitative in nature, involving numerical data, or qualitative, dealing with subjective information such as opinions and attitudes. Thus, individuals pursuing marketing research as a career should have strong backgrounds in computers, math, and statistics, as well as psychology.

Marketing research techniques in the past relied primarily on the measurement of verbal communication via such instruments as surveys, questionnaires, and focus groups. The quantification of consumer responses of what they will buy and what they actually buy sometimes varies. Nonverbal images often elicit the consumers' thoughts and feelings about the things around them more effectively. A new method called ZMET uses pictures rather than words to gain insights into how consumers think and behave. Such companies as Pacific Gas & Electric, AT&T Corp., Coca-Cola Co., Dupont, Eastman Kodak Co., General Motors Corp., Lifetime Entertainment Services, Polaroid Corp., and Reebok International Ltd. have used ZMET to learn customers' attitudes on brands, products, companies, product concepts and designs, product usage and purchase experiences, life experiences, and consumption patterns.[3]

MARKETING RESEARCH ONLINE

Computer technology is having a profound effect on the field of marketing research. Powerful computers enable marketers to compile huge databases in-house to analyze their customers, and Internet-based marketing research offers still more access to information. External information is available through interactive marketing research agencies. Modalis Research Technologies, Inc. was formed through the merger of Socratic Technologies, Inc. and the German research firm Markt & Daten, both specializing in computer-based, interactive research and analysis techniques such as E-mail and Internet surveying. This new company is providing an approach to global marketing research that will focus on developing technological business applications to be used in conjunction with a client's own database.[4]

Another pioneering partnership of Internet marketing research, Greenfield Online, Inc. and Cognitive, Inc., will conduct quarterly surveys entitled *Pulse of the Customer* that will provide information on consumer behavior and current market trends.[5] Additional information is available on Marketing Research Live!, a monthly webcast featuring marketing experts and industry trends presented by ActiveGroup, the leader in market research webcasting, in which viewers can interact with the show's host and guests throughout the presentation.[6]

Access to online information will open many more sources of information to researchers and change to some extent the nature of marketing research. Mass marketing of the 1950s and 60s presented the same message and product to all consumers. This was refined into market segments that divided consumers into smaller groups with common characteristics. Today's database marketing enables marketers to identify very small consumer segments, often on the level of the individual. Individual buying practices and preferences, acquired from warranty cards, sweepstakes, and any form an individual fills out when making a purchase, are entered into huge databases. Powerful software extracts common characteristics of users of specific products. This information is then incorporated into the development of new products, advertising strategies, and every aspect of the marketing process. Databases are continually updated and database-marketing programs have now become "business as usual."

POSITIONS IN MARKETING RESEARCH

Marketing researchers must perform data intensive work, but they must also use logic in their field. Hiring and advancement depends on how effective they are in both areas. According to recruiters, the best jobs are going to applicants who are especially adept in analyzing and reaching narrow market subgroups with greater purchasing power, extreme brand loyalty, or other prime characteristics.[7] Manufacturers of goods or services staff marketing research departments or hire outside firms to do marketing research. The keener the competition, the more important the role that marketing research plays. This role is further determined by the size of the organization and its need for research. In companies with marketing research departments, the director of marketing research usually reports to the marketing manager, who coordinates information from marketing research with technical research and product development. The director of marketing research works with the marketing manager in specifying research projects. These projects are then assigned to analysts who work with other members of the marketing research department in a team effort. The director decides when outside specialists are needed, hires them, and coordinates their activities with those of the internal personnel throughout the research process.

Figure 2.1 shows the positions within the marketing research department or in marketing research firms that are described below. Though a standard career path might be from analyst to senior analyst to assistant manager to manager, in the more organic organizations of today, a new analyst might be introduced into a team with a project already in progress, or given a list of ongoing projects and be expected to contribute to their progress.

Figure 2.1 Marketing Research Department

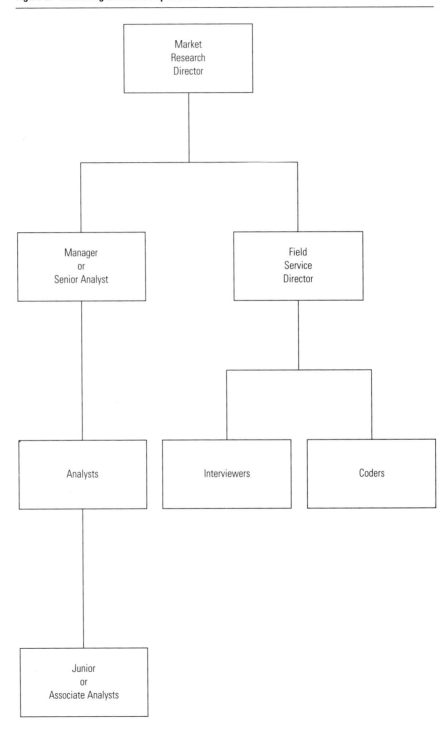

Junior Marketing Research Analyst

College graduates are typically hired as junior or associate analysts. Although entry-level positions may involve such mundane work as handling correspondence and proofreading questionnaires, throughout the first year the junior analyst will also be involved in developing questionnaires for surveys, analyzing data, organizing studies, and writing finished reports. As in every job, the activities assigned to the entry-level worker depend on the worker's ability to handle the tasks and the projects currently underway in the department. Understanding that the first year is a training year, the new worker should use it as a practical learning experience and should be prepared to assume whatever duties are assigned.

Field Service Director

The field service director hires field service personnel, including interviewers and coders, to perform specialized tasks and directs their efforts. Workers in field services conduct interviews by phone or in person, asking questions that have been written by research analysts in charge of a project. Coders or tabulation personnel enter numbers into the computer and run standard types of programs. These programs produce the initial reports that provide the basis for further analysis. Field service and tabulations personnel usually do not need college degrees, often work for minimum wages, and do not normally advance to other positions in marketing research. College students sometimes work part time as interviewers or coders to gain experience in that aspect of marketing research.

   The field service director, on the other hand, is an integral part of the marketing research process. The director may have begun as a junior analyst and been promoted. Depending on skills and performance, the field service director may be promoted to analyst or senior analyst positions. In smaller companies, junior analysts are involved in interviewing and coding. Sometimes field and tabulation work is contracted out to field service firms. The director of field services handles any arrangements, contracts, and communications with these firms.

Marketing Research Analyst

Once junior analysts demonstrate an understanding of the research process and the ability to analyze data and relate conclusions to the specifics of the project, they are promoted to the position of analyst. A marketing research analyst works with managers to gather background material and develop proposals for research projects. Analysts with two or three years of experience work fairly independently on their own projects. Communicating tactfully and courteously with managers regarding pet projects is vital to career success. Sometimes research reveals that certain projects are not viable. The analyst must present these results as thoroughly and professionally as possible. Although number crunching is an important part of marketing research, human relations skills are equally important.

Senior Marketing Research Analyst

After four or five years, successful analysts may be promoted to senior analyst or marketing research manager. Senior analysts may spearhead research projects or function as advisors for other analysts. Although one senior analyst is responsible for each project, the analyst may confer with other senior analysts as needed for suggestions or solutions to problems that arise during the project. Marketing research involves teamwork. The senior analyst supervises the work of junior analysts, coordinates the input of everyone involved on the project, and presents the conclusions. The senior analyst works with, and sometimes under, a research manager. This manager serves in a consulting capacity and, if employed by a marketing research firm, may well have been the individual instrumental in getting the client's business. An important part of the senior analyst's job in marketing research firms is obtaining new accounts and maintaining contacts with clients.

Marketing Research Director

The director of the marketing research department in a company holds the top position and its requisite responsibilities and headaches. In the capacity of director, an individual is the liaison between the department and the rest of the company. Staffing the department, preparing the budget, overseeing all projects, and reporting to the marketing manager periodically are all part of the job. In marketing research firms, the top position—president of the firm—is usually held by the owner or a partner. In this role, bringing in new business is a vital part of the job. The head of a firm is also concerned with satisfying the demands of clients rather than upper-level management. However, whether marketing research is done in a department or by a marketing research firm, the activities performed by analysts are basically the same.

Regardless of the position held, professionals in marketing research work under a certain amount of pressure. An analyst may work on more than one project at a time and face multiple deadlines. Since analysts are assigned total responsibility for projects, the buck stops with them. They are highly accountable for success or failure even though, as in all research, some variables are beyond their control. As an analyst, one is subject to the priorities of others. For example, the marketing manager may dictate the analyst's schedule, requiring the analyst to stop work on one project at a crucial time and take on something else deemed more urgent by upper management. Nonetheless, the work is both challenging and rewarding. Marketing researchers are the pioneers of marketing—exploring new possibilities that sometimes result in revolutionary new products that make life easier or more enjoyable.

OPPORTUNITIES IN MARKETING RESEARCH

Executives in marketing research struggle to find talented young people to fill numerous positions. Not only do today's researchers need statistical knowledge, they must also be skilled in databases, current software, and the Internet. Over the last few years, universities have been attempting to increase the numbers of marketing research students. Companies are competing over graduates of marketing research programs at many universities, including the University of Georgia, University of Wisconsin, Southern Illinois University, and University of Texas.[8] Companies are recruiting students aggressively, and offering more internship and training programs. The Occupational Employment Statistics (OES) Survey for the Bureau of Labor Statistics projects average growth for economists and market researchers with over 27,000 new openings generated from 1998 to 2008. Many of these will go to market researchers, and the supply of qualified researchers may not meet demand as older workers retire and new jobs are created.

Growth in the field of marketing research is a testimonial to its effectiveness. All kinds and sizes of businesses are engaged in marketing research. Hospitals use marketing research to project growth; colleges use it to target potential students and allocate resources among academic areas; and nonprofit organizations look to marketing research to determine who contributes and how best to solicit donations. Large manufacturers of consumer goods staff marketing research departments, but major growth in the field is occurring in the increasing numbers of independent research firms and Internet companies. Some of these firms employ forty or so people, but most are small and often specialize, for example, in educational institutions, hospitals, nonprofit organizations, or a particular type of consumer good or service. Expanding service industries such as financial and business services, cable television, health, and leisure activities also use marketing research firms. Two major retail tracking firms supply information on how well various products are selling and where: A.C. Nielsen Company, which pioneered retail tracking in the 1920s, and Information Resources, which is a relative newcomer to the field. It is wise for those interested in marketing research to develop career objectives with some area of specialization in mind.

Advances in information technology and the commitment of top management to having timely and accurate information have contributed to growth in the field of marketing research. Today, data analysis can be done in a fraction of the time that was required in the past because of more powerful computer hardware and software. Sophisticated multivariate statistical analyses yield information too cumbersome to derive using manual means. This type of analysis takes some of the guesswork out of producing and marketing new products. As both domestic and foreign competition place more pressure on companies to produce successful products, managers will rely more and more on marketing research information to make their decisions.

An undergraduate degree is required for entry into marketing research. This degree may be in any of a number of areas, including statistics, psychology, computer science, marketing, or another business major. The particular major is less important than skills in math, statistics, computers, research design and analysis, and both written and oral communications. As mentioned above, a career objective that focuses on a specific industry in which the applicant has knowledge or experience is helpful. The best chance for a beginner to break into the field is to gain relevant experience as a student, such as interviewing, data entry, involvement in research projects, directed independent study to hone research skills, or an internship in a marketing research department or firm.

Salaries of marketing research professionals vary considerably according to the size of the firm, level of responsibility, geographical location, and other factors that will be discussed in Chapter 11. EUREKA 2000–2001 reports monthly salary ranges from $1,500 to $3,425 a month for entry-level marketing researchers; from $2,300 to $5,165 for experienced researchers; and from $4,900 to over $7,915 for top researchers. Interviewers earn, on average, $1,624 per month.

SOURCES OF INFORMATION

Trade associations are an excellent source for up-to-date career information. Information may also be obtained from the following marketing research organizations:

American Marketing Association
311 South Wacker Drive, Suite 5800
Chicago, IL 60606
Website: www.ama.org

Marketing Research Association
1344 Silas Deane Highway, Suite 306
Rocky Hill, CT 06067-0230
Website: www.mra-net.org

Marketing Science Institute
1000 Massachusetts Avenue
Cambridge, MA 02138-5396
Website: www.msi.org

1. Gibson, Lawrence D. "Quo Vadis Marketing Research?" *Business and Management Practices* 12 (spring 2000): 36–41.
2. Shea, Carol Z., and Carol LeBourveau. "Jumping the 'Hurdles' of Marketing Research." *Business and Management Practices* 12 (fall 2000): 22–30.
3. Catchings-Castello, Gwendolyn. "The ZMET Alternative." *Business and Management Practices* 12 (summer 2000): 6–12.
4. "Two Marketing Research Leaders Join Forces to Form Modalis Research." *PR Newswire*, February 10, 2000.
5. "Post Holiday Study of Online Shopping Planned by Greenfield and Cognitive." *PR Newswire*, December 18, 2000.
6. "Marketing Talk Show to Webcast This Month, ActiveGroup Presents Marketing Research Live!" *PR Newswire*, October 30, 2000.
7. Bass, Carla D'Nan. "Marketing Gets More Sophisticated as Focus Groups Diversify" *The Dallas Morning News*, January 9, 2000.
8. Fellman, Michelle Wirth. "An Aging Profession." *Business and Management Practices* 12 (spring 2000): 33–35.

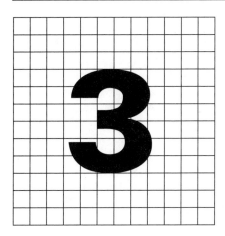

CAREERS IN PRODUCT DEVELOPMENT

Teva, the global leader in performance sports sandals, was founded by a river guide who realized the need for quality footwear that stays on the feet in water. This innovative outdoorsman has received four U.S. patents for his unique designs and his technological innovations help Teva products lead the market.[1] Every year a plethora of fascinating new products hit the market. Multi-fuel automobiles, electronic wallets, smart maps, home health monitors, anti-aging products, next-generation televisions, personalized computers, and thousands of other products are the brainstorms of product development professionals. Products are conceived with particular markets in mind. For example, companies are continually introducing a host of new products to capture the four-to-twelve-year-old market. Clothes, books, video games, movies, television shows, greeting cards, and all sorts of new products designed to appeal to that age group will continue to flow into this steadily expanding market. Many older parents, both working, have more money and only one to two children on whom to spend it, while a dip in the divorce rate suggests greater affluence in two-parent families. It is the job of marketing researchers to document and interpret these trends and suggest new products or marketing strategies to exploit them. For example, Bestfoods recently introduced NutraBlend, a line of four soy beverages to satisfy the taste and nutritional demands of health conscious individuals and families on the go.

Established companies must develop products to compete with the new innovative products constantly appearing on the market. In 1999, for the first time in the twelve-year history of the Product Development and Management Association's Outstanding Corporate Innovator Award, the award went to a major home appliance manufacturer—Maytag Appliances. According to the president of the division, Bill Beer, "[their] approach to innovation is consumer-driven and solution focused. [They] have created a Total Product Delivery System that blends concept generation, product development, and product introduction into one seamless, disciplined, ongoing process."[2] In 2000, cowinners shared the award—Rockwell Collins, Inc., a leader in the aerospace electronics business, and EXFO Electro-Optical Engineering, a small competitor in the fiber-optic test equipment business. These winners are credited with product improvement processes and their ability to transfer creative ideas into successful products.[3] The constant demand for new products is the force that drives product development efforts. Companies try to give consumers what they want, when and where they want it, at a price they are willing to pay. This involves management decisions pertaining to the marketing mix, otherwise known as the four P's: product, place, promotion, and price. Marketing managers assemble product development teams to help make these essential decisions and shepherd a product through the development process. Whether companies can survive and profit in the competitive marketplace depends on the effectiveness of these teams.

THE PRODUCT DEVELOPMENT PROCESS

New product development today has three dimensions: new customer applications, new customer groups, and alternative technologies. One of the most prolific companies in the field of new product development is Rubbermaid. This manufacturer of over 5,000 products introduces new products at a rate of roughly one per day, with nine out of ten successes. This astonishing percentage does not even include the products that are improved versions of other products! Who generates all of these ideas for products? Twenty teams of five to seven people from a variety of departments such as marketing, manufacturing, research and development, and finance. Even top management does its share. Once, two top executives touring the British Museum's Egyptian exhibits returned to the United States with eleven ideas for new products. Along with a variety of kitchen and bath utensils, mailboxes, storage containers, cleaning aids, and tackle boxes, Rubbermaid also offers a variety of products for the youth market including toys, makeup organizers, lunchboxes, and drink bottles. The latter two also appeal to the environmentally conscious.

Product development sometimes involves developing an entire line of products. Black & Decker took notice of the rapid expansion of the Home Depot chain of stores and the popular sitcom, "Home Improvement," and generated billions of dollars in home improvement products. According to a 1999 survey by Competitive Media Reporting, Home Depot ranks fourth among top advertised brands.[4] Even extremely successful companies are confronted with developing new products in order to grow. In 1999, Adidas U.S. footwear sales were $935 million, about 35 percent of the market share for the running shoe category.[5] The following year, sales of footwear and apparel experienced a large drop because of increased competition from popular apparel companies. Adidas has responded with plans to introduce an upscale line of apparel and shoes called *Originals* and a line of expensive sportswear called *Equipment*. These product lines will be a huge risk for the company as they are an enormous departure from the no-nonsense running shoes for which Adidas has come to be known.

The product development process consists of a series of stages. Figure 3.1 shows these stages.

Idea generation. The first stage of product development involves conceiving of ideas for potential products. These ideas come from a variety of sources. Large firms have research and development (R&D) departments whose goal is to keep the firm competitive through the identification of potential new products or the modification of existing ones. R&D is especially vital in high-tech industries that must remain on the cutting edge of technology in order to stay in existence. Other sources of ideas within the company include executives, sales and service personnel, production workers, and marketing researchers. Ideas also come from external sources like trade journals, competitors, and customers. Sometimes inventors approach companies with ideas for products.

Products can be totally new concepts, offshoots from other products, or "new and improved" versions of old products. Cable radio was born from cable television; new Cheerios are crispier to ward off sogginess; and new Wheaties have a milder, whole-grain flavor. Sometimes a new use for an old product can be marketed with positive results. For years horse owners have used Straight Arrow's Mane 'n Tail horse shampoo on their own hair claiming it made their hair softer with more body. Today, Straight Arrow sells two-thirds of its products for human use. Newness from a customer's perspective has been defined as "the degree to which a given product is outside the observer's experience."[6] Whether or not a product is considered new is a function of the individual consumer's perspective.

Idea screening. Ideas must be evaluated in terms of the company's existing products, markets, and resources. Some of the questions that must be addressed include:

- Will the product fit into the company's current product line?
- Can it be sold to existing customers or must new markets be developed?
- Will additional personnel be required to develop the product?
- Must the sales force be retrained?
- Will plant expansion be necessary?
- Can the product be distributed through existing channels?
- How quickly can development costs be recaptured?
- Can the product be advertised and promoted through currently used media?
- Is it able to be protected by patent?

Marketing managers consider many factors during the screening stage, but the basic consideration is whether potential profits will outweigh the costs.

Figure 3.1 The Product Development Process

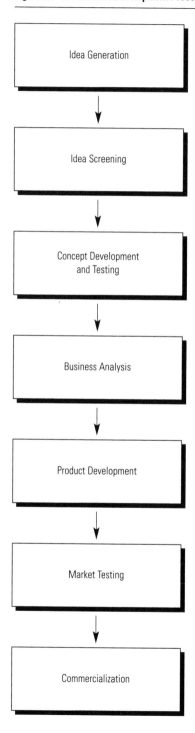

One potential pitfall of introducing new products into any existing product line is cannibalism, a situation in which the new product actually takes sales away from the existing products. When Gillette introduced Sensor, its new permanent razor, its market share in disposable razors declined. However, even though Sensor cannibalized other Gillette sales, its higher price resulted in higher profit margins.

Pricing in today's economy has had an impact on new products. With inflation under control and cost-conscious consumerism on the rise, there is a trend toward producing quality products, with fewer of the extra features that customers don't really value, and offering them at a lower price. Instead of pricing products in the traditional way, adding a profit margin to the cost of producing a product, companies are setting a target price for a new product. Then the product is designed with that price in mind. In the fast food industry, most companies have introduced items priced less than one dollar in order to appeal to younger consumers. The Krystal burger, so popular in the 1950s, has made a comeback with new stores appearing around the country.

Concept development and testing. Ideas that pass the screening process are turned over to marketing research professionals who describe the concept to potential customers and analyze their reactions to it. Do they like it? Would it be useful to them? What characteristics of the product do they like and dislike? Would they buy it? How would they change it to make it better? Demographic, social, and cultural factors of consumers affect how they respond to certain products. Their input at this stage is invaluable to product developers both in improving the product design and identifying the strongest markets for the proposed product. From this research a concept emerges. This product concept then undergoes business analysis.

Business analysis. Many products never go beyond the concept stage because, despite their merits, they would not provide the firm with enough profits to justify development costs. A demand analysis, or a forecast of market and sales potential, must be measured against a cost analysis that considers R&D, production, and marketing costs. If the product still looks good after this analysis, it enters the product development stage.

Product development. Working together, R&D and engineering departments develop a prototype of the product. Only if the prototype tests have the expected outcome in terms of performance, quality, and safety is it slated for market testing.

Market testing. Conventional market testing is done in one or two sample cities chosen because they represent the larger market for the product. Because of the high costs of this type of testing, companies sometimes hire outside research firms to run mini-market tests for certain retail items. These companies arrange to have stores place the product on their shelves to see how consumers like it. Some tests are run in laboratories where subjects are shown ads and promotion materials along with the product. Subjects are taken to mock or real stores, and researchers monitor their buying behavior. Computer analysis of the test results determines whether the product has been received as expected. If so, it enters the commercialization stage.

Despite elaborate testing, problems can arise after a product is introduced. For instance, before Unilever introduced a manganese-based detergent, 60,000 consumers tested the product over a three-month period. Nevertheless, the company was forced to reformulate this powder to combat a charge from an independent consumer organization that claimed its own test showed that cotton clothes are weakened over time by the new detergent. Critics said that Unilever's tests were conducted over too short a time period and with towels made of linen, a very tough fabric. In light of occurrences such as this, each stage in the product development process must be carefully thought out if the product is to be successful.

Commercialization. This is the stage at which the marketing organization operates at full power to develop a marketing strategy for the life of the product. Activities involving production, distribution, sales, advertising, and promotion personnel are coordinated as the product enters production. Technically, this last stage of product development is the first stage in the product life cycle as seen in Figure 3.2. The figure shows how a product is introduced, grows, matures, and declines. When sales of a product start to decline, the company often introduces the "new and improved" version. Sometimes repositioning can revitalize the sale of a product. For example, Procter & Gamble Co. introduced Pampers Phases, disposable diapers with different designs and absorbencies for the four stages of the child's early years. These diapers may actually be identical to the "small," "medium," and "large" Pampers that have been sold for years. However, renaming the product to call attention to its relation to a child's growth stages attracted new customers.

Kimberly-Clark made absorbency improvements to such brands as Kotex, Kleenex Cottonelle, and Huggies resulting in increased market share and higher prices. Gillette Co. spent ten years and $750 million to produce its Mach razor which sells for 35 percent more than its Sensor razor, and U.S. sales grew by 9 percent in the first half of 2000.[7] Implicit in the product life cycle is the continuing need for new products or marketing strategies and the people who develop them.

THE IMPORTANCE OF BRANDS

Anyone who thinks that the appeal of brand names is declining probably doesn't have a teenager in the house. Bolt.com, a global communications site providing free communications services to more than 3.5 million teens between the ages of 15 and 20 around the world, entered into an agreement with The Procter & Gamble Company to develop marketing strategies for a number of its brands and provide brand and customer specific research.[8] Brands have always played an important role in the product offerings of companies. Marketers today consider them strategic assets. Products become brands when consumers associate

Figure 3.2 Product Life Cycle

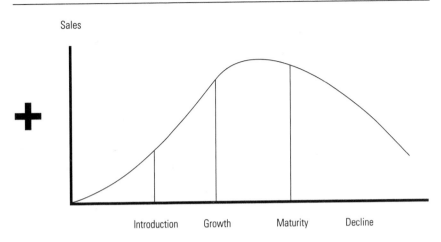

Sales

Introduction   Growth   Maturity   Decline

them with tangible or intangible benefits that they obtain from them.[9] Depending on the current fad, young consumers want clothes with certain labels. Brand names suggest certain styles and qualities; they distinguish products from similar ones and often lend pizzazz to promotion campaigns. Brand identification can help or hurt products. Logos denoting brand names have considerable image appeal and can be a powerful advertising tool. For example, the most frequently requested tattoo in parlors across America is the Harley-Davidson logo. The key to selling a successful brand is the same as for any successful product—understanding its market!

Researchers involved in brand decisions are trying hard to not only define consumer preferences and satisfaction, but also the feelings, emotions, and relationships that they associate with a particular brand. Stephen King once said that factories make products, consumers buy brands.[10] Coca Cola, McDonald's, Procter & Gamble, Gillette, and H.J. Heintz are losing some of their brand power. An analysis of the biggest global brands conducted by Interbrand in 2000 revealed that Microsoft, IBM, Intel, and Nokia were among the top five. While Coca-Cola remained number one, its brand value dropped $11 billion. Yahoo! Inc. has an estimated brand value of $6.3 billion and Amazon.com, $4.5 billion.[11] U.S. consumers are spending less on food and cleaning supplies and more on financial and telecom services. More companies in all industries are using the technology model emphasizing teams, getting products out faster, using database information, and online marketing strategies in product development.

Brand management encompasses how a product is developed, produced, sold, and serviced. Brands, especially high-tech brands, are built using specific characteristics, customer benefits, emotional rewards to customers, quality consistent with promises, and identification of the essential nature of the brand. Successful brand management rewards companies with what they seek most—

loyal customers who are well understood by the company, a good relationship with suppliers and distributors through a promise of value, and a customer's willingness to buy its products even at premium prices.[12] The consumer market today is characterized by eroding product differences. This makes brand identification and loyalty even more important in purchasing decisions. Tracking customer purchases, feelings, and satisfaction is crucial in brand management.

BRAND INFORMATION ONLINE

Numerous firms now offer brand managers news, trends, market data, customer information, and other important information over the Internet. Global Marketing Firm Opinion Research Corporation International, in addition to offering its E-commerce customers information on brand awareness and shopper satisfaction, has launched *e.Tr@ck*[SM], an Internet survey that identified Amazon.com, Barnesandnoble.com, and eBay.com as the most powerful online brands.[13] Brandcities.com offers brand managers a new home page containing the latest best practices, industry news, analysis, and commentary by marketing experts.[14] The Internet's community expert, Talk City Marketing Group, offers online solutions to companies wanting to capitalize on the $700 million E-marketing sector in the areas of customer attraction, conversion, and retention.[15]

Nielsen/NetRatings has entered into partnership with Spectra Inc. to provide brand managers with specialized consumer profile reports to help them identify the best websites to reach a brand's key consumers.[16] Over sixty-five brands and forty-five leading consumer packaged-goods manufacturers now use FreeSamples.com to target consumer groups and offer them free samples over the Internet.[17] Not only do brand managers need help reaching consumers with their products, but also in reaching distributors and franchisees with their advertising messages. BrandMuscle enables manufacturers to set up a system online that enables their distributors and franchisees to customize their ads by selecting from preapproved images, coupons, and customer locations rather than risking a distortion of the manufacturer's message by coming up with their own methods of promotion.[18]

The power of online information and promotion of products for all types of companies, not only Internet companies, is being developed and utilized more every day by companies around the globe. Specific online companies will come and go, but the opportunities offered over the Web will continue to expand and be an integral part of marketing in today's economy.

THE WORK OF PRODUCT AND BRAND MANAGERS

The product or brand manager is assigned a product or product line that is approved for development. Determining objectives and marketing strategies for the product is part of the job description but falls short of describing the work that these managers must perform. Since product managers have no direct authority over personnel in other departments vital to their success, such as advertising or sales, they must be skilled in gaining the cooperation and support of others. It is not unusual for companies to sell products that compete with one another. In this case, a product manager must compete with other product managers within the firm for this cooperation and the necessary resources.

Product managers may be assigned to manage a product through its entire life cycle. Sometimes, however, a new-product development manager is assigned for a product's initial development and test marketing. At the conclusion of test marketing, a product manager will take over and remain in charge of the product throughout the rest of its life cycle. Working under the marketing manager, a product manager must provide the information necessary for top-level management decisions. The responsibilities of product managers are summarized below.

1. Evaluate product testing and recommend whether to terminate development, modify product, or begin campaign.

2. Plan introduction and scheduling of the finished product and packaging with the production department.

3. Provide information and recommendations on price of product in cooperation with marketing research department.

4. Develop sales and profitability forecasts and marketing budgets with finance department.

5. Analyze statistics and recommendations from marketing research to allocate funding for advertising and promotion campaigns.

6. Identify channels of distribution, such as wholesalers, retailers, or direct sales to the public.

7. Work with marketing research and advertising agency to position product; that is, create an image of the product in the minds of consumers as having the attributes that are desired.

8. Coordinate production and promotion of the product.

A less savory role in product management involves recalling products because they pose threats or hazards to consumers. When this happens, a product recall manager is assigned to reverse the marketing channels that are part of the distribution process. Stock is removed from retail shelves, returned to the manufacturer, and either disposed of or repaired. The product recall manager is the person who oversees this entire operation.

PRODUCT MANAGEMENT TEAMS

The product manager has an assistant product manager to help in overseeing and coordinating all activities associated with the product throughout the development process and life cycle. Often the manager and assistant manager head up a product management team consisting of specialists from all areas, including marketing research, R&D, production, advertising, sales promotion, and sales. Sometimes managers choose their own teams; other times specialists from various areas who share an interest in a particular product volunteer to develop that product. Sometimes outside specialists are called in. Product and brand managers should possess a high degree of creativity and widespread interests. Good managers try to foster an environment conducive to creativity in which each team member feels equal and comfortable taking a role in brainstorming and offering ideas. Top management is committed to use whatever resources are necessary to get the job done efficiently and effectively. For this reason, there are no set formulas for personnel use. Rather, personnel assignments may vary from project to project, as the situation requires.

As a product goes into development, product managers and their assistants interact with almost every department in the company. This provides excellent opportunities for learning every aspect of the company business and making contacts that could be useful in advancing to higher positions.

BEYOND PRODUCT DEVELOPMENT

Three important aspects of product development that are planned and carried out with the help of specialists are packaging, distribution, and promotion.

Packaging

Packaging is an unheralded aspect of the marketing process, yet it is as carefully planned as the product itself. A package does more than hold and protect the contents of a product throughout distribution. A package also advertises and promotes the product. Clever packages can give an advantage to one product over a competing one. In addition to being convenient and attractive, a package can be functional; examples include squeeze bottles for margarine, mustard, and ketchup; resealable plastic bags for cold cuts; and tin or plastic containers that can be reused.

The smart product manager involves package designers as part of the development team at the beginning of the project. Engineers and graphic designers generate ideas for packaging with suggestions from other team members including advertising and promotion specialists. Packages may be produced in-house or purchased from outside companies according to specifications from the designers and other team members.

Distribution

Getting a product into the hands of the consumer is a vital part of the marketing effort. A small bakery sells directly to consumers, but what about a large bakery? How do bakeries get the supplies needed to produce their products?

Manufacturers get the materials needed for production from suppliers. Their completed products are usually sent to intermediaries, also called resellers or middlemen. These intermediaries, either individuals or firms, may be retailers or wholesalers. They serve as a link between the manufacturer and final buyers of the product. Careers in retailing and wholesaling will be investigated in Chapters 6 and 7. Producers, intermediaries, and final buyers form what is called a *marketing channel* or *channel of distribution.*

Distribution involves a host of marketing functions, including transporting and storing products, and supplying market information. Since profits depend on the efficient and effective delivery of products into the hands of consumers, distribution is carefully planned as an aspect of product development. As mentioned in the discussion of product screening, having channels of distribution in place is a big plus for any new product. Product or brand managers plan distribution strategy as part of the overall marketing strategy. This strategy is then implemented by a host of distribution professionals.

Promotion

The product manager works with a variety of specialists to best determine how to launch the new product on the market. There are four elements of promotion: advertising, sales promotion, public relations, and personal selling. The extent to which these elements are used depends on the industry and the product. Careers in these areas will be described in Chapters 4, 5, 6, and 7.

OPPORTUNITIES IN PRODUCT MANAGEMENT

Product management is very much like running a small business. For this reason most companies assign entrepreneurial types to the job. In fact, product managers sometimes use their corporate experience to start their own businesses. Large manufacturers hire only MBAs for entry-level positions in product management—assistant product manager. Opportunities in product management in smaller companies and dot-com companies are available to promising candidates with undergraduate degrees. The largest companies offer formal training programs. Other companies have more informal training. In small companies, training is hands-on.

Promotion from assistant to product manager is the usual career track. Some companies producing dozens of brands in various categories have created a higher managerial position called *category manager* to which all brand or product managers in that category report. The category manager, who reports to the marketing manager, plays a vital role in determining marketing strategy for all brands in that product category. Promotions from product management, which is middle-level management, to top management are possible. Corporate marketing management will be discussed in Chapter 8.

According to Occupational Employment Statistics (OES) collected for the U.S. Bureau of Labor Statistics, the broad category of managers, which includes engineering, natural science, and computer and information systems, is expected to grow by 199,000 openings between 1998 and 2008. Though it is impossible to know how many of these jobs will be for product managers, growth in this category is much faster than most, with many of these new jobs in the computer, electronics, and Internet industries. Brand managers are counted within the broad category of advertising, marketing, promotions, public relations, and sales managers for which OES projects 179,000 new jobs between 1998 and 2008, also faster than average growth. The outlook for both product and brand managers appears good.

Because of the broad category of which product managers are a part, salary ranges are quite broad. EUREKA 2000–2001 figures show entry-level salaries ranging from $1,500 to $4,000 per month; experienced workers earn from $3,665 to $7,250 per month; and top pay ranges from $5,000 to over $9,855 per month. Average annual salaries, not considering bonuses and benefit packages, for brand managers in 1998 was $5,001 per month. Salaries of product and brand managers are affected by the importance of the product and brand to which they are assigned. The larger the amount of company resources budgeted for product development, the more important the role of the product manager and the higher the salary. Salaries will vary from industry to industry as well. Other factors that affect salaries and components of compensation packages for managers will be discussed in Chapters 8 and 11. The best chance of landing the most desirable position is to find an internship or cooperative program while still in college. This experience is the key to the best jobs in all areas of marketing.

SOURCES OF INFORMATION

The best career planning sources of information in the field of product management are professional associations. Some of these are listed below.

Product Development and Management Association
236 Route 38 W, Suite 100
Moorestown, NJ 08057-3276
Website: www.pdma.org

Project Management Institute
4 Campus Boulevard
Newton Square, PA 19073-3200
Website: www.pmi.org

American Management Association
1601 Broadway
New York, NY 10019-7420
Website: www.amanet.org

1. "Teva Awarded Utility Patent for Shanking Technology in Its Terra-Fi Sport Sandal." *Business Wire*, February 15, 2000.
2. "Attention Business Editor: Maytag Wins 'Outstanding Corporate Innovator Award.'" *Canada Newswire*, August 20, 1999.
3. "PDMA Announces Corporate Innovator Award Winners." *PR Newswire*, April 15, 2000.
4. Bond, Patti. "Big Orange Spreading Far and Wide." *The Atlanta Journal and Constitution*, October 24, 1999.
5. Gallagher, Leigh. "Bad Fit." *Forbes*, January 8, 2001, 210.
6. Blythe, Jim. "Innovativeness and Newness in High-Tech Consumer Durables." *Journal of Product and Brand Management* 5 (1999): 415–427.
7. Byrnes, Nanette. "Brands in a Bind." *Business Week*, August 28, 2000, 234–238.
8. "Bolt Signs Sponsorship Agreement with Procter & Gamble." *PR Newswire*, September 5, 2000.
9. Gupta, Nirmal. "The Ten Rules of Y2K Branding." *Business Today*, January 7, 2000, 152.
10. Sridhar, R. "Marketing ver 2.100: The New Story." *Business Today*, January 7, 2000, 150.
11. Byrnes, Nanette. "Brands in a Bind." *Business Week*, August 28, 2000, 234.
12. Ward, Scott, et al. "What High-Tech Managers Need to Know About Brands." *Harvard Business Review*, July-August 1999, 85–95.
13. "Amazon.com, Barnesandnoble.com, eBay.com Ranked Three Most E-Powerful Brands on Internet." *PR Newswire*, November 15, 1999.
14. "Brandcities Delivers Web-Based Solutions to Boost Marketers' Success." *PR Newswire*, July 19, 1999.
15. "Talk City Marketing Group's Community Solutions Break New Ground In Online Relationship Marketing: Integrated Suite of Technology and Service Platforms Help Global Brands Turn Consumer Audiences Into Loyalty Networks." *PR Newswire*, November 30, 2000.
16. "Nielsen//NetRatings and Spectra to Provide Brand-Specific Internet Ratings." *Business Wire*, April 13, 2000.
17. "FreeSamples.com Lands Leading National Brands Including Dole, Kelloggs, Planters, PowerBar, S.C. Johnson, Sunsweet." *PR Newswire*, April 28, 2000.
18. "BrandMuscle Puts Power in the Hands of Its Customers." *PR Newswire*, September 20, 2000.

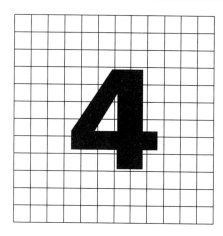

CAREERS IN ADVERTISING AND SALES PROMOTION

Hollywood loves to depict advertising professionals as conniving, though glamorous, individuals operating in do-or-die job situations. Consider the role played by Mel Gibson in the film *What Women Want* in which he suddenly gains the ability to read women's minds. Nike, ready to launch its largest line of women's shoes and apparel in 2001, was happy to play a role in the film that called attention to its new line. Often movie and TV characters mend their unscrupulous ways and turn into likable human beings. Anything can happen in the movies. Ad executives found Miles Drentell's portrayal of an agency leader on the TV show "thirtysomething" among the most accurate.[1] In reality, the advertising field is a highly competitive, stressful, results-oriented one, which is portrayed fairly effectively by the entertainment industry.

Promoting products through advertising and sales promotion devices is evolving as technology opens new avenues to reach consumers. Advertising has undergone major changes and taken advantage of these new opportunities to reach consumers via the Internet and other technologies such as cell phones. Advertising, technology, and marketing experts use approaches such as infomercials that target specific consumer groups; advertising more at live events where consumers are a captive audience; and revising use of both unconventional media, such as in-store advertising, and conventional media, such as newspapers, magazines, and radio, and selling directly to consumers using new media. Then there's viral marketing—a technique in which a message placed at the bottom of an E-mail or an offer passed along by users spreads like the flu. Hotmail, a free E-mail service, put the message, "Get your free e-mail at Hotmail.com?" at the bottom of each E-mail and acquired 11 million users in 18 months.[2] Some companies offer incentives for referrals such as discounts on services and free merchandise. Spotcast Communications offers its customers the option of getting free airtime on their cellular phones in exchange for listening to brief phone ads at the start of a call.[3]

Sales promotion campaigns subtly and effectively influence the American consumer to purchase certain items. Sales promotion, advertising, personal selling, and public relations are the components in a company's product-promotion efforts. How much time and money are spent on each of these components depends on the product itself and decisions made by management. Advertising and sales promotion work together to win customers. Often commercials advertise promotions. The distinction between advertising and sales promotion is that advertising suggests while promotion motivates. Signs that say, "buy one, get one free" or coupons that specify "save 50 cents" motivate consumers to try the product. While advertising may go on for indefinite periods of time, sales promotion is done for a limited time period, normally when a product is first introduced. Often packaged-goods companies spend more dollars on consumer promotions than on media advertising. Giveaways, tie-ins, coupons, and contests are in keeping with the trend of selling to individuals rather than the masses.

THE EVOLUTION OF ADVERTISING

It's interesting to consider the history of advertising and how much it has changed over the years. In the year 1878, before the existence of modern advertising and communications, three defining events occurred. First, a worker churned a batch of White Soap too long, making it light enough to float. Second, an analysis showed the soap to be 99.44 percent pure. Finally, Harley Procter sat in church musing over the words of the Forty-Fifth Psalm, "All thy garments smell of myrrh and aloes and cassia out of ivory palaces whereby they have made thee glad." On Monday, he changed the name of his soap from White Soap to Ivory Soap. The following ad blitz with the familiar accompanying message, "Ivory soap. It floats." created a brand out of a commodity and a resulting soap empire. This story and others are told in the book *Advertising in America: The First 200 Years* by Charles Goodrum and Helen Dalrymple.

Early advertisements established the ground rules for advertising that exist to this day. However, unlike the early ads that communicated a basic selling message in an inventive but forthright manner, the ads of today use more daring techniques to avoid being lost in the barrage of media noise. As a result, many artistically exciting ads leave viewers asking themselves, "What are they selling?" The key then is to make a creative impact and sell the product. Ads that do not result in sales are failures. Even the ads we love sometimes fail to sell products. Consider Taco Bell's Chihuahua, which generated $155 million from Chihuahua merchandise but did not boost sagging food sales.[4] So creative types who opt for advertising as a career must also have a business orientation.

ADVERTISING STRATEGY

Advertisers spend over $2 million for thirty seconds of ad time during the Super Bowl, generating ad revenues of over $100 million for the network airing the game. The ten most-watched television programs in history include seven Super Bowls, two Winter Olympic broadcasts, and the February 28, 1983, finale of the popular show MASH.[5] If the goal is to reach the greatest number of potential consumers at one time, ad spots during the Super Bowl are a safe bet. The quality and provocative nature of these ads is so high that they are talked about after the broadcast almost as much as the game itself. A Yuppie "What Are You Doing?" take-off on the popular "Whassup?" Anheuser-Busch ad aired during the Super Bowl. "Whassup?" not only became a national catchword, but supermarket sales of the Budweiser brand increased 4 percent by mid-September of 2000 compared with a 0.8 percent increase for the previous year.[6]

However, the trend in advertising today is toward textbook-type advertising that stresses value and distinguishes a product from its rivals. This is true even for Apple Computer, whose dramatic, costly, high-concept ads of the early 1980s, designed to produce images linking the product to the customer, made advertising history. This is not to suggest that creative visual artists will be unable to "do their thing" in advertising. Today, the art director carries more clout than his counterpart in copy writing. However, in leaner times, companies are more likely to take a safe approach than to risk hundreds of thousands of advertising dollars on a radical new concept.

An effective advertising strategy is critical to the successful launch of new products. Basically, advertising involves the creation and placement of information designed to increase sales in mass media such as television, radio, newspapers, magazines, and billboards. The designers of a campaign are sometimes influenced by their own circumstances. Kay Napier was working on an ad campaign to promote Procter & Gamble's new drug to treat osteoporosis, Actonel, which initially featured an older white-haired lady watering flowers. Fighting breast cancer herself and using Actinol to ward off osteoporosis, she opted for a campaign that featured a strong athletic woman, The Warrior, practicing yoga with friends and determined to beat the disease with Actonel.[7] The total advertising effort to introduce and stimulate additional sales of a product is called an *advertising campaign* and involves numerous advertising professionals working in a variety of capacities. Often considered the glamour job of marketing, advertising is in fact highly competitive and very hard work. However, for creative individuals who can stand the pressure, the work is both challenging and rewarding.

WHERE ADVERTISING PROFESSIONALS ARE EMPLOYED

Advertising professionals find jobs in advertising agencies, in advertising departments of large companies (in-house advertising agencies), or with mass media as advertising sales representatives. Functions performed are similar in the first two, the obvious difference being that companies promote their own products, while ad agencies promote products for client companies who pay for their services. Both aim for success. The agency that does not come up with a successful ad campaign for a client loses the account. The advertising professionals involved in unsuccessful campaigns sometimes lose their jobs. Most major ad campaigns are created in advertising agencies. One-third of the ad agencies are large, employing over one thousand employees. The other two-thirds are small and often specialize. The vast numbers of advertising jobs are in independent agencies. In-house agencies do offer positions that are comparable in both responsibility and salary, and creative jobs in companies are often less competitive than in agencies.

A position often found in companies that sell goods and services is the marketing communications specialist. Supervised by marketing managers, these specialists act as the liaison between their company and outside firms employed to support marketing efforts such as advertising, sales promotion, and public relations firms. They articulate the company's product strategies and requirements to these firms and report progress and queries on campaigns to the marketing manager. In addition, they may have responsibilities for internal communications.

CAREERS IN ADVERTISING AGENCIES

Advertising agencies usually have four departments: account services, research, creative, and media. Jobs in advertising agencies are divided equally between account support professionals (the suits) including account services, marketing research, and media planning, and creative functions professionals (the creatives). Advancement into account services comes with experience and success in one of the other departments and can lead to management.

The account services department. Just as the product manager oversees every aspect of product development, the account executive plans and monitors all activities in an ad campaign. The proverbial buck stops with the account executive, although all jobs are vulnerable when major ad campaigns are involved. This increases the pressure on the executive. An unsuccessful advertising campaign can result in a product failure for the client and the loss of a major customer for the agency. Because of the vital nature of the work in account services, only experienced individuals need apply. Account executives may be promoted from other areas in the agency or hired from other advertising agencies.

The account executive works with the client, an individual or a company, in planning an advertising campaign. To assess the client's advertising needs, the account executive must be familiar with all of the client's marketing efforts and how the ad campaign will fit in. Communicating the requirements and preferences to the creative and media departments and coordinating all activities related to the account is the responsibility of the account executive. The account coordinator or traffic manager is another vital member of the account services staff. This individual coordinates the work of all four departments throughout the advertising campaign, communicating timetables and monitoring progress.

A trainee in account services, the assistant account executive, usually has experience in advertising and a college degree. Entry-level duties might include handling inquires from clients and other departments, monitoring progress and deadlines in the creative department, communicating with the traffic manager on schedules and ad spots, and in general assisting the account executive. Advancement to account executive may occur after one or two successful years as an assistant. Initially, account executives handle only smaller accounts. They meet with clients to plan a strategy and with other departments to see that it is implemented. They accept or reject ideas from the creative department, and they determine media and ad schedules according to the client's budget.

An assistant account executive who successfully handles ad campaigns and works effectively with clients should be promoted to senior account executive. Senior account executives work on larger accounts and may oversee and advise other account executives, thus gaining the opportunity to hone their administrative skills. The chief position in account services is that of the accounts supervisor or accounts manager. Managers not only oversee accounts, they also actively solicit new clients and advise and train sales staff. These managers are instrumental in bringing new business into the agency and assigning accounts to executives. Acquiring and keeping accounts is what makes ad agencies successful.

The research department. Information collected through consumer research and product testing is often the basis for an ad campaign because it identifies potential users of the product and why it should appeal to this particular market. The research department of an advertising agency functions very much like the marketing research department of any company, but the focus is, of course, on effective advertising. Monitoring trends is a vital function in that trends can determine how products are positioned. For example, the nation's divorce rate is edging lower as baby boomers reach middle age. For this reason it is predicted that more ads will focus on families using products.

An entry-level job as a research project director usually requires a college or graduate degree and experience in advertising or marketing research. Research in an advertising agency means collecting information on how consumers perceive particular products. Conducting primary research involves the development of surveys usually conducted by outside firms and the analysis of survey results. Writing reports containing this analysis and additional information gathered from secondary sources such as the government or trade groups is the job of the project research director. Account services, the creative department, and the media department use these reports in planning the advertising campaign. Once the campaign begins, research focuses on its effect on the intended audience and may recommend changes. Promotion to research account executive depends on talent and innovation. Devising new methods of product and market testing and recommending successful advertising strategies are sure ways to move up in the research department.

Years of successful experience should lead to the position of associate research director, then advertising research director, and finally research department manager. As in all departments in businesses, advancement involves taking on more supervisory and administrative duties. Administrative skills are universally useful, so movement from one department to another is not unusual, particularly for those with a background in research in which problem solving and data analysis are requisite skills.

The creative department. Most of the advertising jobs are found in the creative department, which is composed of copywriters, graphic artists, and layout workers who work in teams under the art director and the copy chief. Figure 4.1 shows the structure of the creative department.

The creative team synthesizes information from the research department, the account executive, and the client to develop the advertisements that will attract the targeted consumers to the client's product. Graphic designers and copywriters are essentially problem solvers, creating distinctive and innovative solutions to the problem of how best to attract and hold the attention of a specific group of people and persuade those people to buy what they are selling, whether it's a product, a service, or a statement of theology.

It is hard to capture the attention of today's magazine flipping, channel surfing public, so art directors are experimenting with every available tool—including type. Letters now leap out of ads and commercials, different typefaces are combined, sentences swim off in all directions. Computers make it easy to create special effects in type styles. Unfortunately, surveys point out that if the message is hard to read, consumers usually ignore it. U.S. agencies added the position of type director, used for years in British agencies, to solve this dilemma.

Most people think of advertising as catchy phrases and gimmicky slogans or jingles. Cleverness and originality are certainly a part of what is required for creative advertising professionals, and humor can be a very compelling sales tool. Ads may also be designed to improve an image such as the General Motors Corporation campaign "Putting Quality on the Road," in which GM both apologized for past quality and deficiencies and boasted about improvements. Sometimes advertising is used to change a product's image and reposition it to attract trendy upscale consumers. Xerox, which many consumers perceived as strictly a copier manufacturer due to strong brand identification, used an ad campaign, "Putting It Together," that focused on the document since its products can now compute, scan, fax, copy—the ultimate in document-producing machines.

Companies often use celebrity spokespeople to convey their advertising message both directly and indirectly. Sports marketers estimate that Lance Armstrong, two time Tour de France winner and cancer survivor, has a product endorsement portfolio worth more than $7.5 million a year from at least sixteen companies.[8] Consider the advertising value of having a player win the U.S.

Figure 4.1 The Creative Department

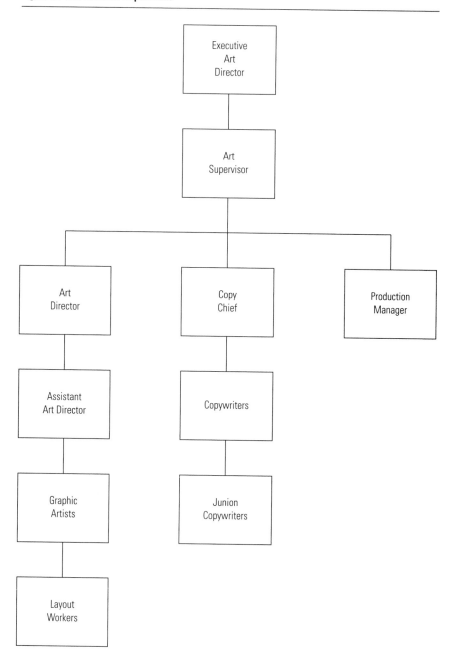

Tennis Open wearing Nike products from head to toe. As part of their contracts, athletes are paid to wear company insignias or logos. Advertisers are capitalizing on the public's desire to identify with celebrities by using products they promote. Stars are well compensated for helping a company sell its products. An important consideration in advertising is the target audience—those who do the buying. Marketing consultants suggest that the use of rugged sports stars and leading men is to appeal to women, who purchase the largest percentage of all men's underwear. Companies targeting young consumers feature hip music from emerging young bands.

Laws to prevent misleading advertising only work some of the time. Like attorneys who slip in remarks that the judge orders the jury to disregard, companies often run misleading ads which have an impact on consumers regardless of the lawsuits that follow. The Hot Rod Association took strong exception to the ad showing a monster truck rolling over five cars, crushing all but the Volvo. Volvo admitted reinforcing the roof of the car with lumber and steel for the stunt. As more commercials attack competing products by name, maligned companies are charging that network review systems are allowing false ads on the air. Advertising industry ethics have often been questioned in the past, and the problem of misleading advertising is unlikely to disappear, especially during hard economic times.

Normally a college degree and, even more important, a portfolio of writing samples and ideas are required for breaking into this highly competitive area. General knowledge of advertising trends and media is also required. Once hired as a junior copywriter, an individual might do everything from answering the telephone to taking part in creative brainstorming sessions. Creativity and the formation of ideas remain a mystery—a combination of knowledge and imagination that can be neither learned nor predicted. The ability to see things in new ways is vital in creative work.

A junior copywriter usually works under a copywriter for a training period. Once promoted to copywriter, one is responsible for writing ad copy, developing concepts for campaigns, and working with artists and layout workers to present finished ads and ideas for commercials. These artists and layout personnel work under an art director to create the visual impact of the ad by selecting photographs, drawing illustrations, choosing print size and type, or sketching scenes for commercials. In addition to preparing magazine and television layouts, they also design packages and create corporate logos, trademarks, and symbols. Production managers oversee the actual printing of ads, filming of commercials, or recording of radio spots. Promotions to senior copywriter, then copy chief are contingent on talent and success. Producing good ads that sell products and make clients happy counts more than years of experience. Like sales, what you produce forms the basis for how you are evaluated. Senior copywriters are assigned the large national accounts that increase the agency's reputation and profits. Copy chiefs supervise other copywriters and work closely with media and account executives in developing ad campaign strategies.

The media department. Once ads are created, they are placed in media selected for the broadest impact. Media professionals develop a media strategy or the proper media mix for best promoting the product. This involves defining the target audience, where they live, and how they can best be reached. Using information from the research department and computers, media planners try to reach the largest number of potential customers in the most cost-effective way.

The new technology only partly explains the movement away from ads delivered to undifferentiated audiences via broadcast television networks and mass circulation magazines and newspapers. The decline in both broadcast network viewing and publications subscriptions combined with rising ad prices has caused marketers to examine alternate media like cable television and the thousands of new special interest publications that have arisen. Basic cable networks offer a highly targeted, often upscale, audience to advertisers at lower prices than the major networks. Regional sports cable networks have been big advertising winners, with ad revenues rising every year.

Marketers have concluded that targeted messages through specialized media are economical and effective. Advertisers want ads addressed to age, income, psychology, and buying patterns placed in media that target specific groups. The desired media packages include combinations of magazines, television programs, books, and videotapes. Technology has produced still other advertising media. Sony Corporation has erected a 23.5 by 32-foot outdoor color video display in Times Square in New York, showing ads as well as news and public service announcements. Internet providers such as America Online and CompuServe run ads along with information. In-store advertising in groceries has gone from ads on fliers, shopping carts, and checkout dividers to television sets mounted over the checkout counter running various ads. Thus, the field of media planning is becoming more complex and challenging.

Candidates for positions in media planning are chosen for their numeric and analytic skills as well as the ability to accept high levels of responsibility. College graduates enter the media department as assistant media planners. Working under experienced planners, beginners are involved in computation and analysis of numbers provided by research or audience ratings done by outside sources such as Nielsen. Advancement to the position of media planner brings far more responsibility. Media planners work closely with account services and sometimes directly with clients in determining the best media mix, that is, how much television, magazine, or other coverage to use. Choosing from many options makes this a challenging job. Adding to the challenge is the need to adhere to the client's media budget, although the media group can make recommendations regarding budget.

Once a client accepts the media plan, media professionals begin meeting with advertising sales representatives from various media and they begin evaluating proposals. Negotiating contracts for advertising space or airtime according to the media plan is the next step. This may be done by media directors and their associates or, in larger agencies, by regional or national spot buyers skilled in negotiating with sales representatives of mass media. After five to ten years experience, media directors can advance to media planners. The media manager, who is in charge of both planning and buying, holds the top job in media.

Media sales reps usually enter the field from positions in media planning, sometimes as spot buyers. Most sales reps work on straight or part commission, therefore they have considerable earning potential. Media sales is high-pressure work, and stress is a factor that should be evaluated by prospective job seekers. Positions in sales are discussed in Chapters 6 and 7.

Along with strong quantitative skills, media professionals must also possess strong communications and interpersonal skills. Functioning as part of a team and acquiescing to clients' wishes and directives from account services require an ability to work well with others and a willingness to compromise. The cost of media is the big-budget item in advertising. Consequently, the pressures and demands on the media department are great. However, media is an excellent avenue into account services.

TYPES OF SALES PROMOTION

Three types of sales promotion contribute to the overall promotion effort: trade promotions, sales force promotions, and consumer promotions. Trade promotions are geared toward intermediaries such as retailers. Manufacturers motivate intermediaries to carry their products by offering such incentives as free goods, dealer sales contests, trade show appearances, and paid cooperative ads. Both manufacturers and retailers offer sales force promotions including sales meetings, contests, and bonuses. The final push to sell the product is through consumer promotions, which include samples, coupons, trading stamps, rebates, point-of-purchase displays, exhibits, brochures, catalogs, sweepstakes, contests, and free gifts-with-purchase. Shampoo with free conditioner, prizes inside cereal boxes, plastic dishes with the dog food—all of these motivate consumers to buy certain products. Low-cost marketing tools such as matchbooks, magnets, and swizzle sticks function as miniature billboards. New in-store marketing techniques that show promise are electronic kiosks, frequent-shopper programs, floor signage, interactive displays, and video.

Some companies use contests to promote their products. Wisconsin-based Puffs sponsored a Tissue Box Design Contest for elementary school students with the theme of "What I Like Best About School" in 1999. The grand prize winner received a $25,000 savings bond for college and a personal computer for home and one for the classroom; additional winners from three different grade levels also received personal computers.[9] Tide, America's best selling laundry detergent, has been conducting contests searching for dirty kids since its 50th anniversary in 1996. The contest in 2000, seeking dirtiest kids and their sidekicks, culminated in judging by a panel and consumers viewing the twelve finalists in *People* magazine and casting votes online or over the phone. People were encouraged by Tide's pledge to donate $10,000 for the first 20,000 votes cast to Give Kids the World, a nonprofit organization that provides Florida vacations to children with life-threatening diseases and their families. Both finalists and winners of the contest were awarded vacations, spending money, Whirlpool washers and dryers, and a year's supply of new Liquid Tide Deep Clean Formula, of course.[10]

Sweepstakes, commonly used by soft drink companies and fast food restaurants, can be used to revitalize brands. Earthgrains enclosed game pieces in packages of its Break Cake snack cakes to be mailed in to the company for the chance of winning a $50,000 prize or a consolation prize of a Break Cake T-shirt.[11] A wilder "Rollin' In It" promotion, cosponsored by Barq's and Tombstone Pizza, invited consumers to roll around in a giant cash-topped pizza, keeping whatever cash stuck to them in addition to receiving Barq's T-shirts and a year's supply of Tombstone Pizza.[12]

The upbeat, try-it-you'll-like-it tone of sales promotion helps to launch new products. A company must succeed in motivating consumers to try the product before it can be market tested. If testing reveals that the product is well received, the company may want to intensify promotion efforts to ensure that it has a winner. The power of promotion efforts and their importance to the success of products cannot be overestimated. Unless the company can stimulate consumers to try new products, even the ones with the best potential are destined to fail because bottom-line profits determine which products remain on store shelves.

POSITIONS IN SALES PROMOTION

Much of what was written about advertising is also true for sales promotion, and many positions are similar. Sales promotion professionals may work for manufacturers, wholesalers, retailers, or sales promotion agencies that operate roughly the same way as advertising agencies. A sales promotion specialist may play a role in product development, both learning about the product and suggesting ways to launch it. Sales promotion is highly specialized and not for beginners. Because of its importance and cost, sales promotion professionals enter the field with considerable knowledge in graphic arts, technical tools, and marketing. Most commonly, sales promotion professionals have had experience in either advertising or sales prior to entering the field.

Creativity is important in designing sales promotion campaigns. Coming up with something new and catchy that attracts consumers to the product is a challenge in a consumer society constantly bombarded by new products and promises. Demonstrators and models show the product to the public in shopping malls, grocery stores, and at trade shows. Graphic artists and copywriters work together to produce packaging for samples, coupons, buttons, T-shirts, and other promotional items. Layouts, materials, sizes, and shapes are all part of the creative process. Sales promotion efforts are planned and coordinated by a specialist assigned to the product.

Just as an account executive works with a client in an advertising agency, a sales promotion specialist provides the same services. Considering a client's product, sales promotion budget, and marketing research collected both for the product and similar products, a sales promotion specialist plans a campaign and directs a creative team in producing items needed to carry it out. A good specialist possesses research abilities, administrative skills, and creativity.

ADVERTISING AND PROMOTION ONLINE

Marketers today can accomplish a wide variety of tasks online from narrowly targeted advertising, to distributing and tracking coupons, to accessing information on agencies, designers, and advertising campaigns, to exploring career opportunities in their fields. Some methods commonly used for online advertising are the following: E-mail ads, which target specific customers and have the best response rate; banners, which comprise 50 percent of online ad revenue but whose click rate has been declining; skyscrapers, the skinny ads that run down the right or left side of a website whose click rates can be seven times that of banners; streaming video and audio, in which ads are inserted into music and video clips as consumers listen to them more like TV; effectiveness tracking, which places tiny files called *cookies* on viewers' computers enabling the tracking of consumer behavior after seeing ads; and minisites, pop-ups, and interstitials, which features ads that burst onto screens without sending users to different sites.[13]

Online advertising has not grown as quickly as predicted because of concerns of traditional marketers that formats for ads were not appropriate for their products and results of online ads were difficult to measure.[14] The potential is definitely there for attracting marketers. Consider that Yahoo reaches 60 percent of Net users around the world and 70 percent of employees of the 500 largest companies, tracking 166 million users with personal information on 55 million of them, who have been differentiated into narrow targeted groups as small as 17,000.[15] That's pretty impressive.

Advertising executives responded to a 2000 survey by The Creative Group that the position of web designer would be the fastest growing creative position over the next three years. More and more companies are offering consumers user-friendly, one-on-one websites to build brands and customer loyalty. An *Advertising Age International* special report showed www.campbellsoup.com to be the best website among forty companies surveyed, offering everything from recipes to company financial information.[16]

Warp10 developed the adsGallery.com website to offer marketers a free directory of thousands of major ad agencies, independent designers, and hundreds of portfolios of advertising campaigns.[17] Marketer.com offers an exchange that posts requests for advertising proposals by brand managers that can be accessed and responded to by ad agencies, direct marketing and public relations firms, stock photographers, and trade show companies.[18] These are but a few of the sites providing this type of information to marketers.

OPPORTUNITIES FOR ADVERTISING AND SALES PROMOTION PROFESSIONALS

Advertising generates billions of dollars for media each year: television, $35 billion; radio, more than $15 billion; magazines, about $12 billion; and the Internet, roughly $5 billion.[19] So despite complaints about a proliferation of ads in all media, the field will continue to offer many opportunities to job seekers. Though types of ad campaigns, specific uses of the media, and the amounts spent on advertising may vary, companies will continue to use advertising to communicate with customers and consumers will want to see ads that introduce new products. A slowdown in the economy and volatility in the dot-com sector suggest that fewer dollars will be spent on high-profile expensive advertising campaigns in the immediate future.[20] Less expensive alternatives such as newspaper, magazine, and radio advertising, direct selling, and public relations are likely to benefit from a recession economy.

The largest ad agencies are owned by diversified parent companies and are somewhat insulated from downturns in the economy. The top three ad agencies today are WPP, with an estimated $6 billion in revenues in 2000, Omnicom, with $5.9 billion, and Interpublic Group, with $5.6 billion.[21] Intense competition both in domestic and global markets will sustain growth in advertising and promotion efforts. Large advertising agencies offer comprehensive services often including more sophisticated marketing research and in-house production facilities to clients. Smaller firms are willing to negotiate on commissions and are often more flexible in their approach to satisfying their customers' needs. Most of the top U.S. agencies are headquartered in New York and maintain satellite offices around the world.

The African-American and the Hispanic-American markets form two huge consumer groups that have received much focus in the advertising world. Target Market Research Group, a Hispanic marketing research firm, and Zogby International, a polling firm, are conducting surveys that measure the growth and importance of the Hispanic-American market. African-American ad agencies have capitalized significantly on the multibillion dollar urban market with an understanding of the attitude of hip-hop culture and its appeal to all youth. In 1999, two of the top-three African-American owned agencies aligned with large general market firms. In the advertising field, mergers are common among agencies of all sizes and ethnic orientations. Online advertising geared to the African-American community hasn't grown as fast because of racial misconceptions. A 2000 survey conducted by Cyber Dialog revealed 4.9 million African-American Web users, half of which were under the age of 30 and over one-third were college graduates with an average income of $58,000.[22]

In Canada, almost every major global agency has an office in Toronto. Advertising and sales promotion in Canada differ from U.S. work in both magnitude and style. With a population only 10 percent the size of the U.S. population, agency accounts are considerably smaller. More specific government restrictions limit what can be said on broadcast media about both products being offered and their competitors. Those seeking employment in Canada should be fluent in both English and French. A free booklet entitled "So You Want to Be in an Advertising Agency" can be obtained by writing the Institute for Canadian Advertising at 30 Soudan Avenue, Toronto, Ontario M4S 1V6.

According to an Occupational Employment Statistics (OES) survey, new openings will number 179,000 between 1998 and 2008 in the category for advertising, marketing, promotions, public relations, and sales managers—this is faster than average growth. Although demand is strong for advertising and sales promotion executives, the new graduate enters a highly competitive job market. College preparation for entry-level jobs is oriented toward the development of job-specific attributes gained through courses in advertising, journalism, and business. Recruiters are looking for students with skills in advertising coupled with courses in areas such as history, humanities, and anthropology. Advertising graduates must be prepared to enter a competitive, global environment that will require a broader perspective.

OES predicts that demand for artists and multimedia occupations will also grow at a faster than average rate, with 143,000 new openings projected over the years 1998 to 2008. Commercial art directors are included in the category of designers, except interior designers, and is expected to increase by roughly 140,000 new jobs—also a faster than average growth rate. The same growth rate is true for copy editors, who are grouped with writers and editors, including technical writers. Advertising salespeople grouped in the category for other sales and related workers can expect average growth with 1,436,000 new openings between 1998 and 2008.

It isn't unusual for advertising and sales promotion professionals to change jobs from corporate to agency settings and vice versa. Agency executive compensation levels are often tied to the size of the agency's billings, while corporate executive compensation varies with performance-tied bonuses. In general, entry-level salaries throughout the advertising industry are low. The training and experience gained by beginners, however, enables them to more effectively compete for jobs higher up the ladder. Salaries increase considerably with advancement and are contingent upon experience, job duties, and the size and prestige of the employer. The following figures are from EUREKA 2000–2001.

Job Title	Monthly Salary
Advertising director	
Entry pay	$1,750 to $2,600
Experienced pay	$1,250 to $3,750
Top pay	$4,125 to over $12,080

Advertising account executive

Entry pay	$996 to over $3,750
Experienced pay	$1,210 to over $4,165
Top pay	$2,500 to over $5,765

Artist

Entry pay	$1,175 to over $2,000
Experienced pay	$1,550 to over $2,955
Top pay	$2,000 to over $3,880

Copy editor

Entry pay	$1,500 to $2,000
Experienced pay	$2,100 to $3,500
Top pay	$3,700 to over $5,500

Annual salaries for the middle 50 percent of designers, including commercial art directors, range from approximately $20,000 to $40,000. Annual pay for sales agents, including advertising sales, can range from $12,000 to over $54,000. These ranges are so large because salaries are dependent on the specific job and a host of other variables. More useful salary information on what recent college graduates are being offered is discussed in Chapter 11.

SOURCES OF INFORMATION

Numerous books and periodicals about advertising and sales promotion are available. Of all career areas in marketing, these fields are described in the most detail. In addition, trade associations offer a large amount of general information on the fields and professional development. Below is a partial list of resources.

Publications

Two popular advertising periodicals are *Advertising Age* and *Brandweek*, weekly publications found in most public and college libraries. There are dozens of excellent periodicals for advertising professionals. Those interested in media can read *Broadcast Week* and *Marketing and Media Decisions*. Job seekers can use directories such as *Roster and Organization of the American Association of Advertising Agencies* and *Standard Directory of Advertising Agencies*.

Associations

Some associations for advertising and sales promotion professionals that offer information are listed below. Some offer student memberships at a discounted rate.

The Advertising Club of New York
235 Park Avenue South, Sixth floor
New York, NY 10003

The Advertising Council
261 Madison Avenue
New York, NY 10016-2303
Website: www.adcouncil.org

Advertising Research Foundation
641 Lexington Avenue
New York, NY 10022
Website: www.arfsite.org

Advertising Women of New York
153 E. 57th Street
New York, NY 10022

American Advertising Federation
1101 Vermont Avenue Northwest, Suite 500
Washington, DC 20005
Website: www.aaf.org

American Association of Advertising Agencies
405 Lexington Avenue, 18th floor
New York, NY 10174-1801
Website: www.aaaa.org

Association of Promotion Marketing Agencies Worldwide
750 Summer Street
Stamford, CT 06901
Website: www.apmaw.org

Promotion Marketing Association of America
257 Park Avenue, 11th floor
New York, NY 10010-7304
Website: www.pmalink.org

Radio Advertising Bureau
261 Madison Avenue, 23rd floor
New York, NY 10016
Website: www.rab.com

Retail Advertising and Marketing Association, International
333 North Michigan Avenue, Suite 3000
Chicago, IL 60601
Website: www.ramarac.org

Television Bureau of Advertising
3 E. 54th Street
New York, NY 10022
Website: www.tvb.org

Internships

The American Advertising Federation listed above is an excellent source of advertising internships offered by many of its members. A membership list may be obtained by writing the organization. Although all companies listed do not sponsor interns, many do. Internships in advertising are offered during summer, winter recesses, and regular school terms. Because internships are such a desirable way to break into the field of advertising, applicants face stiff competition. It is therefore recommended that applicants develop a good resume, target an area of specialization in which they would like to work, and use all available resources to get leads on internships.

 1. McCarthy, Michael. "Admen Behaving Badly Flourish in Movies, on TV Stereotypes Smarmy with Hearts of Gold." *USA Today*, December 26, 2000, 5B.
 2. Kelly, Erin. "This Is One Virus You Want to Spread." *Fortune*, November 27, 2000, 297.
 3. Kellner, Thomas. "Connected." *Forbes*, August 21, 2000, 115–116.
 4. Blakeley, Kiri. "Drop the Chihuahua." *Forbes*, August 21, 2000, 60.
 5. Johnson, Greg. "Super Bowl Commercial Buyers Put It on the Line." *Los Angeles Times*, January 18, 2000.
 6. Wells, Melanie. "It's a Mad, Mad, Mad Ad World." *Forbes*, December 11, 2000, 194.
 7. Nelson, Emily. "How Women Warriors Replaced Gardeners in P&G Ad Campaign." *The Wall Street Journal*, February 21, 2001, A1, A10.
 8. Horovitz, Bruce. "Armstrong Rolls to Market: Gold Cyclist Makes $100,000 for 1-Hour Speech." *USA Today*, May 4, 2000, 1B.
 9. "Tissue Box Design Contest Offers Wisconsin School Kids Chance to Win $25,000* for College and Computer." *PR Newswire*, November 17, 1999.
10. "Tide Unearths America's Dirtiest Kids and Their Sidekicks: National Search Discovers Six Dirty Duos." *PR Newswire*, October 24, 2000.
11. "Sweet $50,000 Offered in Break Cake® 50K Frenzy Sweepstakes Promotion." *PR Newswire*, January 20, 2000.
12. "Barq's Root Beer Lovers Will Be 'Rollin' in the Dough' This Summer, Literally and Figuratively." *PR Newswire*, May 17, 2000.
13. Green, Heather, and Ben Elgin. "Do e-Ads Have a Future?" *Business Week*, January 22, 2001, 48-49.
14. Green, Heather. "Net Advertising: Still the 98-Pound Weakling." *Business Week*, September 11, 2000, 36.
15. Hardy, Quentin. "The Killer Ad Machine." *Forbes*, December 11, 2000, 169–170.
16. Dietrich, Joy. "Maria Puoti." *Advertising Age International*, May 1, 1999, 46.
17. "Warp10's adsGallery.com Selected as Premier Showcase for IBM's HotMedia." *Canada NewsWire*, May 3, 1999.

18. Clark, Philip B. "Pairing Marketing Buyers, Providers." *Business and Industry* 85 (August 28, 2000): 20.

19. Alsop, Stewart. "Give Commercials a Break." *Fortune*, January 22, 2001, 50.

20. "Advertising." *Business Week*, January 8, 2001, 102.

21. Sellers, Patricia. "Ad Man on Fire." *Fortune*, July, 10, 2000, 161.

22. Hayes, Cassandra. "Media Meltdown." *Black Enterprise*, June 2000, 180.

CAREERS IN PUBLIC RELATIONS AND CUSTOMER SERVICE

The public relations (PR) industry has been growing at a surprising rate, with a 30 percent increase in 1999 alone. The U.S. Department of Labor Statistics predicts that PR jobs will increase on average faster than all other occupations, with 76,000 new jobs created from 1998 to 2008. Factors contributing to this increase are the growth and complexity of business, the globalization of the economy, expanding media opportunities, and the Internet boom. The Council of Public Relations firms predicts that the $3 billion industry may well double in size by 2003 because of the demand created by the Internet for new types of information services.[1] Studies show that changing jobs is expected of employees and usually required for advancement and pay increases in the public relations field. Because of this high turnover rate, headhunters have contacted almost 70 percent of the PR professionals in agencies and corporations over the past year. Many individuals seek performance-based pay, a compatible work environment and corporate culture, and a boss they can respect.[2]

Low prices and profit margins, the high cost of implementing new technology, better educated and more price-conscious consumers, and expensive advertising and sales promotion make the use of public relations and customer service more vital to the success of a company. Any good businessperson knows that it costs a lot less to hold onto customers than to acquire new ones. Building relationships is the way to keep customers loyal. Public relations is the means to build a positive relationship with the community, and customer service is the way to foster a long-term relationship with the individual customer.

THE ROLE OF PUBLIC RELATIONS IN PROMOTION

Public relations involves the creation of publicity. Publicity is information about the company and its products that appears in the mass media; it falls into the category of news. Unlike paid advertising, publicity may be good or bad, it may originate with the company or the media, and it is aired free. Organizations today depend on goodwill not only from consumers who make up the markets for their products, but from the public at large. The actions of an organization in producing and marketing a product sometimes have a wide impact. Therefore, public relations professionals must understand attitudes and concerns of various groups, such as government agencies, environmentalists, consumer advocates, stockholders, and residents of communities in which companies build their plants.

Lobbying for favorable legislation and against unfavorable legislation is one of PR's numerous activities. Monitoring and advising management of societal changes that could affect future actions of the firm is another. The basic mission of PR is building, maintaining, and improving the public image of the firm. A positive public image helps to promote the company's products. Because of the national attention to worthwhile causes in the 1990s, many companies are engaging in "cause marketing." For example, many companies are helping to sponsor and publicize fund-raising events for causes such as shelters for the homeless, AIDS prevention and cure, and breast cancer research.

THE NATURE OF PUBLIC RELATIONS WORK

Entry-level work as an assistant account executive in public relations includes acquiring information from a variety of sources and maintaining files, both fundamental parts of the research process. With experience, PR professionals begin to write press releases, executives' speeches, and articles for both internal and external publications. Other duties, such as working with media contacts, planning special events, and making travel arrangements for prominent people are all part of PR.

Promotion to public relations account executive depends on the demonstrated ability to generate innovative ideas, to work well with others, and to communicate effectively with groups of employees, media representatives, and clients. Once promoted to account executive, the professional works independently and directly with clients, planning and executing a public relations campaign strategy. Advancement to public relations account supervisor carries with it responsibility over major campaigns and the budgets for groups of accounts. The director of account services in a public relations firm, often an owner or partner, typically oversees campaigns and budgets and works to attract new clients.

Public relations, like advertising and sales promotion, is campaign oriented. When a campaign is launched, it is often necessary to work overtime. Meals with clients and frequent travel are sometimes on the agenda. Deadlines and pressures are implicit in this type of work. A small group of PR professionals even specialize in restoring battered images of celebrities at rates that can reach $2,500 per month. The satisfaction derived from creatively planning a campaign and enjoying its success is worth the irregular hours and extra demands for those with the proper temperament and disposition for PR work.

Public relations firms and professionals may specialize in any of a number of areas:

• *Consumer affairs* involves fielding inquiries from customers, preparing educational materials, and addressing consumer safety and quality issues.

• *Government relations* requires lobbying for or against certain legislation, researching and presenting information to the staff of government agencies, and recommending legislation useful to the company.

• *Investor relations* is a field in which the PR professional serves as a liaison between the shareholders and the company, preparing reports, planning meetings, handling shareholder inquiries, and encouraging investment.

• *Employee relations* requires the PR professional to coordinate communications between employees and management by producing in-house publications and arranging meetings, seminars, and conferences.

• *Community relations* involves organizing programs, activities, tours, classes, and publications for schools, civic groups, neighborhood associations, and interested individuals.

• *International relations* includes researching foreign customs, preparing information to be used in foreign countries, entertaining foreign visitors, and introducing the company abroad.

• *Media relations* requires writing and placing press releases, producing clips for television, organizing press conferences, and arranging appearances of company executives.

The type and amount of public relations effort in any of these areas depends on the size and nature of the organization. A small staff working under the director of public relations usually does in-house PR. Larger firms may have two PR departments—one for internal company PR and one for product promotion. In PR firms, the number of employees and their titles depend on the size of the firm. Like advertising, good PR work begins with research to determine a client's goals and how best to accomplish these goals in light of the competition. This is true whether a client is a business or a political candidate. The areas above have many activities in common that typify public relations work: research, writing, media placement, public speaking, and event coordination.

EDUCATION AND PERSONAL REQUIREMENTS

What attributes do top PR professionals possess? They include problem solving, sociability, persuasiveness, a sense of urgency, self-confidence, assertiveness, empathy, and stamina. Individuals who possess many of these traits and have excellent verbal and written communications skills may successfully enter the field of public relations. Applicants hold degrees in a variety of areas—communications, business, and liberal arts, among others. Most colleges offer programs in public relations through the communications department. However, a recent survey showed that 95 percent of public relations employers are willing to hire and train nontraditional PR candidates with transferable skills. In fact, the Council of Public Relations Firms hosted a "non-communications" public relations job fair in Boston on May 4, 2000 to attract college students in non-communications careers to the field of public relations.[3]

OPPORTUNITIES IN PUBLIC RELATIONS

Public relations professionals are hired by many types of organizations including businesses, nonprofit organizations, trade associations, government agencies, colleges, prominent individuals, large advertising agencies with PR departments, and public relations agencies that serve a wide range of clients. Some public relations agencies are quite large. Weber Shandwick Worldwide, for instance, is the largest global and U.S. PR agency, with 1999 revenues of almost $300 million and 2,500 employees in sixty-eight offices in twenty-two countries.[4] Creativworks, a retail-based network of advertising and marketing agencies, entered into a partnership with PR Newswire, thus enabling the company to offer its clients a full range of public relations services including targeted release distribution, Internet monitoring, and mass fax distribution.[5]

Most PR agencies are small, employing fewer than a dozen people. Agencies located in smaller cities offer excellent job opportunities. In Canada, major agencies are located in the large population centers of Ontario and Quebec. In general, because of the size of Canadian markets, both projects and budgets will be smaller than in the United States, and bilingual applicants are given preference.

Spring Associates Inc., a leading executive recruiting firm specializing in public relations and marketing communications, discovered through a recent survey an increase in opportunities for entry-level staffers in both the consumer and high tech industries. The survey further revealed that women outnumber men in high tech PR by 8 percent.[6] Demand for new recruits is so great that entry-level salaries are being raised at a higher rate than executive salaries. According to a survey conducted by *PR Week*, public relations salaries rose nearly 8 percent in 1999, more than four times the national average, with comparable growth expected for 2000.[7] Salaries in public relations positions vary according to size of the agency, experience, geography, industry, and area of specialization. In medium and large-sized agencies, salaries rose more than 12 percent. Typically, each five years of experience yields $10,000 more in salary. In general, salaries are highest in the East, followed by the Midwest, West, and the lowest salaries are in the South. The average national salary for PR specialists in 1999 was $66,979. The highest average salaries were earned in New York City, $84,566; Washington, D.C., $82,547; and Los Angeles, $78,707. The following table shows average salaries by industry sector:

Financial services	$78,939
Utilities	74,507
Retail	73,730
Industrial/manufacturing	73,537
Food and beverage and Professional services	72,296
High tech	69,957
Government	56,415
Nonprofit	54,047
Education	49,836

The highest paid specialty area in public relations is crisis management, with an average salary of $90,110; the second highest is investor relations, with an average salary of $88,051. The 1999 *PR Week* salary survey further revealed that self-employed PR professionals earned the highest average salaries, $85,644; followed by corporate executives, $76,421; and finally agency executives, $69,833. The average salary of an executive vice president of a large PR agency is $205,905, while MBAs in public relations are being hired right out of school at $60,000 a year.

Those interested in PR work should try to get some meaningful experience prior to college graduation. Work experience and knowledge in an area of specialization or a specific industry are very helpful. Internships during college or as a first job after graduation provide an excellent way of gaining experience. Employers use interns' skills to screen them for potential entry-level hiring. Because of the importance of internships and the competitive nature of the job market, many colleges and universities require internships for graduation. Job applicants should prepare a portfolio of PR projects on which they have worked. The college campus affords many opportunities for involvement in such projects, such as joining the staff of the campus newspaper, radio, or television station or becoming active in student programs. Working as a volunteer on political campaigns is also excellent experience.

SOURCES OF PUBLIC RELATIONS INFORMATION

Internships in public relations are available but are not easy to get. Professional public relations associations sometimes sponsor internships and will also know of opportunities for beginners. A Career Press publication, *Public Relations Career Directory*, contains articles, job-finding information, and entry-level openings in the United States and Canada.

Associations such as the ones listed below enable PR professionals to share information, take part in seminars and conferences, and remain up-to-date on trends that impact their careers.

Canadian Public Relations Society
Canada Newswire
750 W. Pender Street, Suite 1003
Vancouver, BC V6C 2T8
Canada
Website: www.cprs.ca

Institute for Public Relations
University of Florida
P.O. Box 118400
Gainesville, FL 32611-8400

International Association of Business Communicators
1 Hallidie Plaza, Suite 600
San Francisco, CA 94102
Website: www.iabc.com

International Public Relations Association, U.S.
433 Plaza Real, Suite 275
Boca Raton, FL 33432
Website: www.ipranet.org

National Black Public Relations Society
6565 Sunset Boulevard, Suite 301
Hollywood, CA 90028

National Investor Relations Institute
8045 Leesburg Pike, Suite 600
Vienna, VA 22182
Website: www.niri.org

Public Affairs Council
2033 K Street, Suite 700
Washington, DC 20036
Website: www.pac.org

Public Relations Society of America
33 Irving Place, Third floor
New York, NY 10003-2376
Website: www.prsa.org

Women Executives in Public Relations
P.O. Box 7657 WEPR FDR Station
New York, NY 10150-7657
Website: www.wepr.org

Public relations periodicals offer a wealth of information regarding the current happenings in the field and advice to professionals. Job openings are also published in the classified ad sections of various publications such as *PR Week*, *Public Relations Journal*, *Public Relations Quarterly*, *Publicist*, *Public Relations News*, *Public Relations Review*, and *PR Reporter*. Some or all of these can be found in public or university libraries.

Press Access, Inc. offers a website (www.pressaccess.com) for PR professionals that features information on recent media changes and appointments, studies and surveys, upcoming news and events, and important industry links to resources.

THE IMPORTANCE OF CUSTOMER SERVICE IN TODAY'S ECONOMY

Many people assume that search tools on the Web make it so easy to compare prices that price would become the most important factor in choice. This is not true. A recent MIT study conducted by Erik Brynjolfsson, associate professor of the Sloan School of Management and codirector of the Center for eBusiness, revealed that only 47 percent of consumers bought items from the lowest priced seller. Customers were willing to pay higher prices for high-quality service and innovation. The factors impacting sales were the choice of sites previously visited, advertising, name recognition, shipping time, and finally price. The study showed that in business-to-business markets, customers use the supplier with the best service.[8] A 1999 survey conducted by Jupiter Communications, a research firm focusing on how the Internet and other technologies are changing traditional consumer industries, reported that 42 percent of the top-ranked websites are taking longer than five days to respond to customer E-mail or failing to respond at all.[9]

We live in a service-oriented economy. Even when selling goods rather than services, courteous and helpful customer service adds value to the product and contributes significantly to customer satisfaction. Today's marketers realize how important customer satisfaction is since retaining customers is less costly than finding new ones. One Fortune 500 firm reorganized sales teams into "customer-focused teams" including specialists on order management, system configuration, and personnel, in addition to establishing customer care centers and global support centers to help field personnel solve customers' problems.[10] For this reason, most companies are attempting to build long-term customer relationships. Satisfied car buyers tend to buy the same brand over and over. This can add up to hundreds of thousands of dollars over the span of a lifetime.

Given that one never gets a second chance to make a first impression, sales personnel are being retrained to think in terms of customer service. Providing the kind of useful information that helps customers make intelligent choices in terms of their individual needs and values is the current orientation to selling and keeping customers. In business-to-business marketing, suppliers are in effect entering partnerships with customers by helping them to improve processes, reduce costs, and deliver quality. Successful customers buy more products from their suppliers.

Global competition, technological change, and shifting customer demands place pressure on companies to retrain their personnel to function in a dynamic marketplace. Using the new technology and focusing more on solving customers' problems are two issues at the heart of this retraining. To retain a customer base, companies must find out what their customers' needs are, how well they are being met, and design products and services accordingly. Another key is employee retention. Experienced employees better understand what customers need, and satisfied employees help customers buy more.

Smart companies respond to customer complaints with a prompt personal reply sometimes accompanied by coupons and free products. Customer complaints can be a valuable source of information for product development. Sincere responses to complaints and follow-up corrective action can generate positive word-of-mouth advertising. Adding value to products and services by providing better customer service is an effective competitive strategy for every company. Some ways to add value include learning a customer's business and suggesting new ways to improve it, providing a guarantee, offering some free service, and providing a customer with options.

CUSTOMER SERVICE SALES

Customer service is everybody's job—sales personnel; support staff who handle orders and problems; distribution personnel; and managers who assess customer needs, plan products to satisfy them, and train and maintain satisfied employees. The position of customer service representative exists in many companies. We speak to them to set up accounts for banking, cable television, or any of our utilities. These representatives deliver the company's product or service to its customers in addition to providing information and answering questions. They are the troubleshooters who handle complaints, expedite repairs and maintenance, and explain warranties. These positions require courtesy, helpfulness, competence, and product knowledge. In the past, customer service was considered an area that supported sales. In today's service-oriented economy, this rapidly growing field has been accurately renamed—customer service sales.

Roughly 75 percent of all jobs in the United States are in a services industry. Customer service sales personnel include call center employees, stock brokers, travel agents, insurance agents, real estate agents, property appraisers, health club operators, and owners of beauty salons, day care centers, and housekeeping services—to mention only a few. All of these individuals are selling services. Many positions require the use of computers and knowledge of industry-specific software. All require excellent communications and marketing skills. Consider the millions of customers who call banks every day for product information and financial help. Banks must use customer-focused technology in call centers, adapt Internet and E-commerce capabilities, and hire and train customer service–oriented personnel.

Cooperative programs between businesses and communities are yielding qualified customer service professionals. For example, a new training program in customer service for job seekers over 40 years old called Operation ABLE of Michigan is being funded through a grant from Ameritech and the SBC Foundation. This program is designed to help mature workers acquire customer service skills while providing businesses with skilled employees in the office, retail, and service sectors.[11] Another cooperative arrangement involves 800 Support, a supplier of technical and customer support services, and Southwestern Oregon Community College, the state of Oregon, the Oregon Economic Development Department, the city of North Bend, and Coos County. A call center established by 800 Support in North Bend offering 500 new technology and customer service jobs was staffed with area residents that the college trained for free. In addition, state economic development officials provided funding assistance for equipment and leasehold improvements for the company.[12]

Customer service representatives are included in three different Occupational Employment Statistics (OES) categories, so numbers of new jobs are hard to estimate, but all categories are projected to have faster than average growth. Annual salaries in 1998 for customer service representatives ranged from approximately $19,000 for entry-level workers to over $28,000 for top workers, with average annual pay for all representatives at approximately $24,000.

TECHNOLOGY AND CUSTOMER SERVICE

Well-trained customer service representatives aided by new technology can easily solve customer service problems. Customers today can choose how they want to shop—freestanding establishments; E-mail; Web pages; and call centers. Regardless of how orders are placed, businesses must provide customers with a consistent level of service. In an effort to do this, they have invested heavily in enterprise resource planning and customer relationship management systems to solve customer service problems and to target their top clients since usually 20 percent of a business's customers generate 80 percent of its profits. Digital Consulting Inc. hosted The Customer Relationship Management Conference in 2000 to allow over forty-five exhibiting companies to display solutions such as systems, software, and network products that support and make customer relationship management more efficient.

MarketSoft Corporation was one of eleven companies nominated by *Computerworld* in the Customer Relationship Management category as one of the "Top 100 Emerging Companies to Watch in 2001." The company was recognized for its eMarketing applications, developed to help business-to-business and business-to-consumer companies create, fulfill, and measure demand to improve marketing impact and profits.[13] Servicesoft Technologies, Inc. developed Servicesoft eCenter to provide integrated solutions that address all customer service demands on the Web, including self-service, E-mail management, and live interaction.[14] Customer intelligent enterprise (CIE) is a new technology trend related to customer relationship management (CRM) systems but goes one step further. While emphasizing rapid communications and interaction with customers, it gives call center employees the responsibility of helping to solve customers' problems rather than just cataloging their complaints.[15]

To learn more about customer service, contact the International Customer Service Association, 401 N. Michigan Avenue, Chicago, IL 60611-4267.

1. "Should You Launch a PR Career in 2001?" *PR Newswire*, January 2, 2001.
2. "Heyman Survey of Senior Level U.S. PR Executives Shows Job-Hopping Seen as Necessary to Advance in Field." *Business Wire*, November 8, 2000.
3. "The Council of Public Relations Firms Kicks Off First 'Non-Communications' Job Fair in Boston" *Business Wire*, April 27, 2000.
4. "Interpublic Refocuses P.R. Brands Around Global Practice Growth Opportunities: Weber Shandwick Worldwide Rises to No. 1 in U.S., World." *Canada NewsWire*, September 19, 2000.
5. "Creativworks Adds Best-of-Class Public Relations Resource to Portfolio of Services." *PR NewsWire*, January 15, 2001.
6. "Surprise: Women Outnumber Men in High-Tech PR, Salary Report Finds." *PR Newswire*, May 3, 1999.
7. "PR Means Pay Raise: Industry Paychecks Grew 8% in '99—Nearly Four Times the National Average, Outpacing Growth of Advertising Salaries." *Business Wire*, March 30, 2000.
8. Solomon, Melissa. "Service Beats Price in Web Shopping, MIT Study Finds." *Computerworld*, June 19, 2000, 28.
9. "Web Sites Failing at Customer Service" *TeleProfessional* 12: 16.
10. Sharma, Subhash, et al. "A Framework for Monitoring Customer Satisfaction: An Empirical Illustration." *Industrial Marketing Management* 28 (May 1999): 231–244.
11. "Operation ABLE of Michigan to Announce 'Ameritech Customer Service Training Program for Mature Job Seekers' at September 26 Open House." *PR Newswire*, September 22, 2000.
12. "800 Support to Land Its Third Technical Call Center in the Pacific Northwest." *PR Newswire*, July 27, 1999.
13. "*Computerworld* Selects MarketSoft as One of the Top 100 Emerging Companies to Watch in 2001." *PR Newswire*, December 11, 2000.
14. "Servicesoft Technologies, Inc. Delivers Industry's First Complete E-service Solution" *Business Wire*, June 14, 1999.
15. Scannell Boston, Tim. "New Customer-Service Hybrid on the Horizon." *Computer Retail Week*, July 16, 1999.

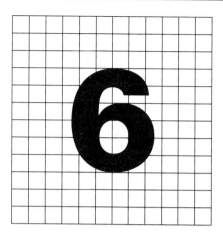

CAREERS IN INDUSTRIAL, WHOLESALE, AND DIRECT SALES

Many college students aren't aware of the varied career opportunities in selling and sales management and many even have negative perceptions of sales careers. A 1999 study of business students in the United States, New Zealand, and the Philippines showed that students preferred a career in marketing management, describing sales as stressful, boring, and pushy.[1] This is not good news for industrial marketers and sales managers, particularly in global businesses. Though business schools offer undergraduate courses in personal selling, most business students don't enroll in them. Students are therefore not always aware of the opportunities in industrial sales. It has been debated whether or not courses in personal selling focus on key skills needed in the industrial marketplace. A recent survey of practitioners and educators indicated that a stronger emphasis should be placed on communications, critical thinking, and reasoning skills, and that techniques such as individual student projects and presentations, discussions of selling issues and business events, guest speakers, role-playing, and team projects are vital in teaching these skills.[2] Industrial marketers are working to establish better relationships with business schools and are offering more internships. Through sales-related internships and participation in professional sales organizations, students can gain valuable experience and determine whether sales is a profession they would like to consider.

The 1990s witnessed a metamorphosis from the in-your-face salesperson to the "relationship manager." Though successful sales personnel require many of the same attributes as in former years, they now require a few more in addition to a new orientation. Solving problems and satisfying customers as well as generating sales volume are measures of success. Some companies have begun to tie salary to customer satisfaction and to eliminate commissions in favor of bonuses based on corporate profits. This sales approach requires more training, knowledge, and teamwork than in previous years. Computer companies such as IBM and pharmaceutical companies such as Merck & Company, Inc. both use this approach.

The area of sales is a vital part of the marketing function. Sales professionals have a key role in moving products into the marketplace. After production, manufacturers may opt for any or all of the available channels of distribution by selling products directly to customers, to retailers, or to wholesale intermediaries. The area of wholesaling is unfamiliar to most consumers who deal only with retailers. Wholesaling is the link between the manufacturer and the retailer who sells to consumers. Basically, wholesalers sell to everybody except ultimate consumers—including retailers, other wholesalers, and manufacturers. Although manufacturers may sell their merchandise directly to retailers, wholesaling intermediaries provide many valuable services both to their suppliers (manufacturers) and to their customers (retailers). Often it is more cost effective for a manufacturer to sell goods at a reduced price through wholesalers who incur the costs of sales personnel and warehouse expenses. Manufacturers who sell directly to final consumers often use the services of self-employed manufacturers' representatives.

A growing trend is direct marketing. This term refers to a variety of methods of non-store selling, including direct selling, direct response retailing, database marketing, direct mail, and telemarketing. Both manufacturers and retailers use direct marketing. This chapter focuses on careers in sales for those interested in employment by manufacturers, wholesalers, and direct marketers. Careers in retail stores will be discussed in the following chapter.

THE SALES PROFESSIONAL

Regardless of employer or type of sales (industrial, wholesale, retail, or direct), sales professionals perform the same functions. Selling can be hard work with long and irregular working hours, extensive travel and entertaining, and sometimes reluctant and unwilling customers. Sales representatives must possess self-confidence, persistence, and optimism. Excellent communication skills are essential because sales representatives are also expected to be technical advisors, educators, and trainers. A vital part of the art of selling is persuading potential customers that a product will best solve their problems and satisfy their needs. People want clean carpets, not vacuum cleaners; peace of mind, not insurance; happy children, not toys. Therefore, to sell a vacuum cleaner, insurance, or any other product, a sales rep must persuade the potential customer that this product is the best on the market to satisfy his or her needs.

The hard sell is definitely out of vogue. The effective salesperson today helps the customer to buy. This is done through first asking questions to better understand the customer's wants and needs and then providing information that helps clarify these needs. Then, while making recommendations, the sales rep talks about company products and their advantages to the customer. The emphasis remains on the customer. Customer service is the concept behind successful selling, which requires individuals who are genuinely interested in their customers, want to see them happy with their choices, and can effectively communicate this desire. Sales representatives are selling themselves and their companies, not merely their products. This is how they generate repeat business. They are gaining customers, not merely making one-time sales.

THE NATURE OF SALES WORK

Sales representatives perform numerous activities, including some of the following:

1. Setting goals, planning, and making schedules.
2. Identifying and contacting prospective customers.
3. Maintaining contacts with current customers and anticipating their needs.
4. Planning and making sales presentations.
5. Reviewing sales orders, scheduling delivery dates, and handling special details.
6. Maintaining up-to-date records and reports.
7. Handling complaints and problems.
8. Monitoring the competition.
9. Learning new product information and marketing strategies.
10. Evaluating price trends and advising customers.

Time management is crucial to successful selling. Sales representatives must carefully allocate their time among the above activities. Some industries have cycles with peak selling periods during which more time must be spent on customer contact. Slack periods provide time for record keeping, following up with customers, researching new products, and so forth. The steps of the selling process are:

Step 1: Prospecting

Step 2: Preparing the pre-approach

Step 3: Approaching the prospect

Step 4: Making the sales presentation

Step 5: Handling objections

Step 6: Closing the sale

Step 7: Following up

Today, sales representatives use technology to make their jobs easier. Sales automation is a huge industry. Prices of laptops and notebooks are decreasing, making them affordable for more and more sales representatives. Personal computers and notebooks aid in record keeping and information gathering. Car and cellular telephones save time. Fax machines and communication networks get information to customers and the home office quickly. Generating and responding to leads is enhanced by such technology as broadcast voice mail that can leave as many as 50 personal messages per hour, predictive dialers that deliver a prerecorded message to thousands of consumers each day, and Internet technology offering systems containing customer demographics and credit information that can respond to thousands of leads, track the results, and provide options for follow-up.[3] Using technology is essential for sales professionals to compete in the marketplace of today.

A college degree in marketing or an industry-related area is preferred for many positions in sales, but is not always necessary. However, promotions to company manager are usually given to those with college degrees. The professional association, Sales and Marketing Executives International (SMEI), offers a certification program for sales and marketing managers. The SMEI Accreditation Institute verifies educational experience, knowledge, and standards of conduct of candidates for certification.

INDUSTRIAL SALES AND WHOLESALING

Computers and communications networks are having an impact on the relationship between suppliers and buyers. Computer links between suppliers and targeted consumers are beginning to eliminate the need for some intermediaries. However, database technology has helped retailers and wholesalers alike to determine exactly what products are needed and when. The stocking practices of both have become more efficient and less wasteful. In the computer industry, where items become obsolete very quickly, products must be sold immediately. A computer that can process many transactions per second and is equipped with a fax modem is used to accomplish this. Various opportunities and work environments exist for those in industrial sales and wholesaling. Sales representatives are employed by manufacturers or merchant wholesalers, or they can be self-employed as manufacturers' agents or wholesale dealers.

Company sales representatives and managers. Sales representatives employed by companies are given training and expense accounts. Depending on the company's products, they may sell to wholesalers, retailers, directly to industrial users, or to individuals through manufacturer's outlet stores. Inside sales workers stay in an office and solicit or take orders by phone. In addition, they process orders and monitor inventory. Field sales workers visit customers to solicit sales, provide information on new products, or to render technical assistance. Some sales representatives offer services to retailers such as checking and reordering stock or suggesting promotion and display techniques. Industrial or electronic equipment sales representatives may install and service what they sell. Sales representatives work with purchasing agents and other buyers for customer companies.

In large companies, sales representatives work under a district manager and, if promoted, may hold that position themselves. Levels of management within companies differ according to the organization's size and structure, but most sales representatives work under a sales manager. The sales manager establishes training programs, assigns territories, and defines goals for the sales reps. The ability of sales managers to train and develop others is one key to their success and subsequent promotion. District sales managers may work under product or brand managers, depending on the company and its product offerings. Sales managers get information from dealers and distributors on customer preferences. In addition, they project future sales and inventory requirements for the geographical area that they have been assigned. The district sales manager reports to the regional sales manager, who reports to the national sales manager, who works directly with the vice-president of marketing. Not all sales representatives aspire to climb the corporate ladder, preferring the autonomy of sales work to the headaches of management. It is not unusual for effective sales representatives on commission to earn more than managers whose salaries are fixed.

Purchasing agents. Companies usually employ purchasing agents to obtain items they need for production. Purchasing agents also are employed by local, state, or federal governments. Normally specializing in one product or group of products, they shop for the best quality at the lowest price. Purchasing agents arrange payment and delivery of products according to their employer's specifications. They may deal with company sales representatives, manufacturers' agents, or wholesale intermediaries.

As a field, purchasing is becoming more complex. Those interested in purchasing as a career should study such topics as negotiation, purchasing law, international purchasing, federal regulations, computerized purchasing, and product liability. There is a need for more purchasing programs in schools across a broader geographical area. Well-trained purchasing professionals are in high demand.

Manufacturers' agents. Manufacturers' agents or representatives are independent business people who may sell one product, a group of similar products, or a variety of products to different types of customers. Normally they are assigned a territory in which only they can sell the company's products. The manufacturer pays a commission for each sale. Manufacturers' representatives have no expense accounts or big company benefits as do company-employed sales representatives. What they do have is total freedom—the advantage of being self-employed. Manufacturer's representatives are seasoned sellers, not beginners. The best preparation for obtaining permission from a company to sell its products is to first gain experience by working as a company-employed salesperson within the industry. Once accepted as a manufacturer's representative, an agent provides an invaluable service to manufacturers who cannot afford to maintain a company sales force. The manufacturer pays a commission only on products sold, but ambitious agents can earn sizable salaries if they are excellent salespeople.

Merchant wholesalers. About 80 percent of wholesaling establishments, accounting for slightly over half of wholesale sales, are classified as merchant wholesalers. These independently owned businesses purchase products from the manufacturers and resell them to other manufacturers, wholesalers, or retailers. Usually referred to simply as wholesalers, those specializing in industrial products are often called industrial distributors, and those specializing in consumer products are called jobbers. Wholesalers may provide a range of services, including ordering, shipping, warehousing, and credit. They may stock a variety of products, one or two product lines, or, in the case of specialty wholesalers, part of one product line.

Wholesale dealer. Basically, the job of wholesale dealers, also called merchandise brokers, is to bring buyers and sellers together. These dealers or brokers may work for either the buyer or the seller. Whoever employs them pays the commission. Typically, wholesale dealers will find the products specified by their client companies at the best price, add their commission (roughly 30 percent), and give the customer the quote. Although the dealer may negotiate deals on behalf of the client, the client decides whether to accept or reject these deals. If employed by manufacturers, the dealers will find a customer for the manufacturers' products and negotiate a deal. Brokers handle both goods and services. Most individuals deal with real estate, insurance, or investment brokers.

Other wholesalers. Numerous other types of wholesalers provide similar wholesaling services as well as career opportunities for those interested in wholesale sales. Included are petroleum bulk plants and terminals, which resell petroleum products to industrial users, retailers, and other wholesalers. Farm product assemblers buy grain, cotton, livestock, fruits, vegetables, and seafood from small producers to sell in large quantities to central markets or food processing companies. Public warehouses store bulk shipments and break them up for resale in smaller quantities. Resident buying offices offer a collection of merchandise such as apparel from various manufacturers for resale to small retailers who cannot afford to go to market frequently.

Trade show planning and management. Industry trade associations or trade-show management organizations sponsor trade shows that enable producers, wholesalers, retailers, and customers to view and discuss their industry's product offerings. These shows vary in size and function and take months, and sometime years, to organize. Because of their increasing popularity over the past ten years, trade show planning and management offer many new marketing career opportunities. In addition to the exposition or show manager, marketing professionals from marketing research, advertising, sales promotion, and public relations are employed to make the trade show a success.

Show managers have a variety of responsibilities. First, they must arrange lodging, meals, and transportation for show exhibitors. Second, they must arrange for preparation of exhibit directories, organize display space and equipment, and hire temporary personnel such as receptionists and clerks to work before and during the show. Third, they must direct the marketing effort to attract exhibitors and attendees to the show and provide them with information. In addition to job opportunities with industry trade associations and trade-show management companies, exhibitors hire marketing specialists to determine shows in which to participate, to plan the exhibit, and to staff it with sales personnel. Exhibitors may also hire exhibit designers, who specialize in creating the most positive image for a company and its products, and contractors who build the booth.

E-COMMERCE AND ONLINE TECHNOLOGIES

Electronic commerce has experienced tremendous growth over the last few years, yet it still only accounts for a small fraction of all sales. The Connecticut-based Gartner Group estimates that business to business E-commerce, which was $145 billion in 1999, will grow to $7.29 trillion worldwide in 2004.[4] One of the impacts of electronic commerce will be to lower prices as online markets allow suppliers to easily submit competitive bids for contracts with manufacturers. Some economists feel that the reduced costs of doing business online will help control inflation. The complex relationships that big manufacturers develop with suppliers are likely to continue as before, but the use of online technology to reduce costs of doing business and to improve efficiency is the way of the future.[5]

Distribution Utilities Online, or DUO[SM], by iSwag.com offers distributors Web-based order management tools that enable them to manage such things as product offerings, processing orders, order histories, tracking products, and many other aspects of distribution.[6] Entrade Inc., based in Chicago, offers various industries commercial Internet clearinghouses. Online sites enable customers to see parts and products, distributors to store large amounts of product information, and companies to offer technical support. Marketing Database Associates, Inc. developed mda-energyleads.com™ to allow energy service providers to monitor sales leads, compute returns, and measure responses to their marketing programs and sales follow-up efforts.[7]

Although manufacturers are wary of upsetting the retailers who sell most of their products, the Web is too tempting to ignore. It offers them an opportunity to showcase their products, establish direct links with consumers, and increase profits. Websites have been developed for brands such as Timex, Clinique, Sony, General Electric, Ford, Mattel, and Polaroid. According to a fall 1998 Ernst & Young survey, 15 percent of manufacturers were selling online, up from 9 percent the previous year.[8] Though this trend is likely to continue, online consumer commerce will always be dominated by retailers who conveniently bring different manufacturers' products together on one website. GMBuyPower.com is a website that sells GM products; however, in light of consumer preference for independent dealers on the Web, GM has recently proposed forming a company called AutoCentric that would offer information and sales opportunities for other makes and models of cars over the Web, allowing dealers who purchase shares in the online company to offer inventory at special online prices.[9]

THE GROWTH OF DIRECT MARKETING

The Spring & Summer 2000 Sears Catalog offered to Canadian consumers contained 1,240 pages of product photography and description. Today it is online with 2,018 Web pages and 50,000 images.[10] The tremendous growth in direct marketing or non-store selling is another testimony to the desire of the American public to shop quickly and easily. From the company standpoint, direct marketing lowers selling costs because selling via mail, telephone, or computer is less expensive than in-person sales calls. Mail-order shopping is nothing new to small-town residents. Mail-order houses such as Sears and Montgomery Ward began with the expansion of railroads and the postal service after the Civil War, offering rural shoppers convenience and low prices. Today, a variety of methods are effectively used to reach shoppers in towns and cities of all sizes: direct selling, direct response retailing, database marketing, direct mail, telemarketing, and E-marketing via the Internet. The growth in direct marketing has created many career opportunities for professionals both in sales and other areas of promotion such as advertising and sales promotion. Direct marketing is conducted by firms who sell products from other companies, and firms and individuals who sell their own products. Every imaginable type of product is sold through direct marketing—apparel, plants, computers, insurance, travel services, portraits, aluminum siding, pay-per-view television, even steamy love novels personalized with customers' names used for the major characters.

DIRECT SELLING

Direct (door-to-door) selling, also called direct retailing, is almost an American tradition. Many of us have sets of encyclopedias, the *Great Books of the Western World*, and vacuum cleaners to prove it. For years we have watched Dagwood Bumstead wage war on door-to-door peddlers who are both resourceful and determined. Direct selling is defined as the marketing of products directly to customers through personal explanation and demonstration in their homes or businesses. Direct sales representatives receive training in ingenious ways to sell a product, including demonstrations. Avon, the largest cosmetics firm in the world, employs a huge number of door-to-door representatives. They work autonomously, setting their own timetables. Other well-known companies include Amway Corporation, Kirby Company, Mary Kay Cosmetics, Inc., and World Book.

Although actual door-to-door selling is decreasing as more and more women begin to work outside the home, party-plan selling, institutionalized by Tupperware, is still going strong. Party-plan salespersons recruit hosts or hostesses to give parties at which they demonstrate and sell their products, sharing some of the profits and gifts with the host.

Requirements for direct selling careers include a pleasant, outgoing personality and a lot of initiative. A high school education with some courses in speech and business is helpful. Although a college education is not required, courses in business, marketing, psychology, advertising, and sales promotion would be beneficial.

DIRECT RESPONSE RETAILING

Marketers advertise their products in magazines, in newspapers, on radio, on television, and on the Internet. In direct response retailing, also called direct response advertising, an address or phone number is given so that consumers can write or call to place an order. Credit cards and toll-free numbers have enhanced this type of marketing. Often, marketers hire service bureaus that handle calls and take orders.

Approximately ten years ago, the home-shopping industry was born. Home Shopping Network and QVC Network sell such items as jewelry, home products, consumer electronics, apparel, and toys to millions of viewers. Computerized voice-response call-handling systems are used to process calls efficiently and cost-effectively. The home-shopping networks also began to use such marketing tools as celebrity endorsements and direct mail coupons.

DATABASE MARKETING

Database marketing is revolutionizing the way we perceive selling today. Sometimes called relationship marketing or one-on-one marketing, it involves the collection of volumes of information on groups or individuals. Information collected over the Internet, from coupons, warranty cards, sweepstakes, or given at the time of purchase is combined with other information that is part of publicly recorded information such as real estate records. Through sophisticated statistical techniques and high-powered computer technology, this information is refined to identify specific consumer groups who share characteristics such as income, brand loyalties, and buying practices. These groups or individuals are then targeted as possible markets for new products, recipients of coupons, and entries to lists of potential customers that may be used, sold, or rented. For example, companies sell or rent lists of students, their schools, and their home addresses from kindergarten through graduate school. Based on demographic data such as income, number of people in the household, geographical location, homeowners, or college major, lists can be tailored for specific company needs. Sources such as birth and wedding announcements, magazine and catalog subscription lists, and professional membership directories are used to create mailing lists. One way to ensure being on numerous lists is to make a purchase via the computer, through the mail, or to be on a catalog subscription list. For example, consumers who purchase plants through the mail from one company are very likely to receive a catalog or brochure through the mail from another company offering plants. The same is true for clothing or any other product.

TELESERVICES

Once a marketing tool, teleservices has grown into a profession able to capitalize on developments in telephone technology and changes in the economy. Marketing done over the telephone called telemarketing or, more recently, teleservices, has experienced a dramatic increase since the 1970s. Some businesses have in-house telemarketing departments, but most use the services of telemarketing agencies organized much like advertising agencies and direct mail firms. Teleservices is sometimes used with direct mail or other advertising techniques. Inbound telemarketing involves receiving calls from prospective customers as a result of direct response retailing. These calls may be to place orders, seek information, or make complaints. In outbound telemarketing, the marketer contacts prospective customers by phone to solicit sales. Telemarketers work from prepared scripts written to keep the consumer interested while encouraging purchase of the product or attempting to arrange a sales presentation. Telemarketing may be done from a call center or a home phone, making it a convenient job for people with disabilities or for parents of small children. Phone companies and companies offering warranties on products recently purchased use outbound telemarketing regularly. Many firms use computerized phone systems that automatically dial a phone number and play a recorded message.

Teleservices professionals are in demand and turnover is great despite efforts to make call centers more attractive and comfortable. Telemarketing directors or call center managers oversee marketing operations, negotiate telephone contracts, and incorporate new telecommunications technologies into the marketing effort. Telesales representatives are trained on the job. A pleasant telephone voice and the ability to handle rejection graciously are required since most calls do not result in sales. To alleviate the high turnover rate, this growing young industry is developing career paths for its employees to include such positions as team leader, recruiting specialist, training specialist, and operations manager. These specialists hire, train, and motivate new personnel, prepare reports, make projections, and coordinate operations. Promotion to telemarketing director or call center manager usually requires several years of experience and a college degree in business, marketing, or a related area.

In addition to vacations and health plans, many teleservices firms offer other benefits such as 401K plans, individual or team bonuses, profit sharing plans, medical reimbursement plans, perfect attendance awards, tuition reimbursement, and matching contributions for charitable giving. Salaries vary geographically and depend on whether the calls are consumer or business-to-business calls and whether they are outbound calls or inbound calls. According to a 1998–1999 salary study conducted by the American Teleservices Association, some average salaries are as follows:

Teleservices representative	$30,300
Teleservices manager	$45,000
Teleservices director	$66,300

Source: J. Scott Thornton, "How Benefits Build the Future," *Business and Management Practices*, June 1999, vol. 12, no. 6, pp.63–68.

CATALOG RETAILING

Among the thousands of companies that offer merchandise for sale through catalogs, the top non-store catalog retailers of 1999 include Damark International, Hanover Direct, Lands' End, Lillian Vernon, Micro Warehouse, and Neiman Marcus Direct.[11] Growth in catalog sales peaked in the late 1970s and early 1980s. Although growth has slowed, the catalog business is still growing at a faster rate than in-store retailing. Catalog sales enable shoppers to select items from a vast array. Most catalog companies have liberal return policies. More and more products will be offered in new and innovative ways through catalog retailing. Though catalog retailing primarily employs order takers, there are key positions for buyers, advertising professionals, and marketing managers.

DIRECT MAIL

Direct mail is one of the fastest-growing segments of the direct marketing industry. It includes catalogs sent through the mail, promotional letters, and other materials offering products for sale. Direct mail is used to produce leads, inquiries, orders, or an increase in store traffic. Another benefit of direct mail is that it enables producers to determine exactly who is buying their products. Advertising campaigns can then target identified markets. Specialized direct mail firms and advertising agencies offer direct mail services. In both cases, account, research, creative, and media departments work together to develop the direct mail campaign. The campaign focuses on established and potential customers. Companies may purchase targeted mailing lists from list brokers. List management firms compile, sort, update, and rent lists of names. They employ list managers, sales personnel, computer personnel for data entry, programming, and analysis, and research personnel.

OPPORTUNITIES FOR SALES REPRESENTATIVES

The Occupational Employment Statistics (OES) survey for the U.S. Department of Labor has projected average growth and 1,436,000 new jobs for sales representatives from 1998 to 2008. Business services salespeople will grow faster than average with a projected growth of 147,000 new jobs from 1998 to 2008. The growth and success of direct mail is due in large part to being able to target market segments through the use of database marketing. That these databases are an invasion of privacy and cause a veritable paper blizzard of advertisements for those who order by mail cannot be denied. Similarly, unsolicited phone calls, even to unlisted telephone numbers selected at random, are becoming a nuisance. As of December 2000, thirteen states have passed laws allowing people to put their names on do-not-call lists, but so many organizations are exempted, including companies with whom people already do business, that they only reduce telemarketing calls about 15 to 20 percent.[12]

It is likely, considering the demographics of the American public and the trends in lifestyles, that direct marketing will continue to grow at a faster rate than in-store marketing. Although fraudulent offers and questionable product claims cause consumers to be somewhat wary, products offered at reduced prices that can be ordered simply by dialing a toll-free number or over the Internet are very attractive.

Sales representatives' earnings are very difficult to project. Sales representatives may be paid on straight commission, thus income is a percentage of sales made. It can fluctuate greatly depending on peak and trough selling periods within the industry, the economy, and the ability of the salesperson. Sometimes sales personnel are paid a set salary plus a commission on sales. Some are paid a straight salary. Employers normally pay at least some commission as an incentive for sales representatives to generate more sales and thereby benefit directly from their efforts.

Employers offer numerous types of bonuses. The most common bonuses are given for meeting sales quotas. Project launch bonuses are common in pharmaceutical and high-tech sales if a large percentage of the targeted accounts sign on. Bonuses are given for account penetration where sales are increased in under-penetrated accounts or product lines. Manufacturers offer sales personnel bonuses for increasing intermediary participation in product training or gaining information about competitor business. Calling on personnel outside of purchasing who might influence a distributor's buying decision might be awarded with a bonus. Many companies use bonuses as incentives. Insurance and real estate companies tend to favor contests and prizes such as trips. Trips have become popular as incentives among many Fortune 500 companies as well.

Sales representatives must sell in order to earn their commissions. Employers normally offer beginners a salary or salary plus commission until they reach a predetermined sales level. Another common practice is to let beginners draw income against future commissions. If they are unable to generate sales, sales representatives quit or get fired. Those who cannot sell cannot support themselves in a sales profession.

In areas such as real estate, insurance, and financial services sales, annual income can be very large. However, in these areas only the top 10 percent normally make a lot of money. If an individual has the ability to be in this top percent group, there is no limit to income; it usually rivals or exceeds that of top management.

According to EUREKA 2000–2001, average pay for sales representatives in 1998 was $50,496. Sales supervisors earned $57,300. Business services salespeople in financial services earned $61,776, while those in the general business services category earned $40,248. Telemarketing salaries vary by level of experience, industry, and region. Entry pay ranged from $996 to $1,150 per month, while top pay was over $2,475 per month. In 1998, call center managers averaged $4,358 per month, regional directors averaged $6,275 per month, and telemarketing directors had a range of $6,116 to $7,150.

SOURCES OF INFORMATION

Information on wholesaling and industrial sales can be obtained from the following professional associations:

Association of Industry Manufacturers Representatives
222 Merchandise Mart Plaza, Suite 1360
Chicago, IL 60654
Website: www.aimr.net

Manufacturers' Agents National Association
23016 Mill Creek Road
P.O. Box 3467
Laguna Hills, CA 92654
Website: www.manaonline.org

National Association of Wholesaler-Distributors
1725 K Street NW, Suite 300
Washington, DC 20006
Website: www.wawmeetings.org/am2000/

National Association of Business and Industrial Saleswomen
5107 North Mesa Drive
Castle Rock, CO 80104

National Association of Catalog Showroom Merchandisers
186 Birch Hill Road
Locust Valley, NY 11560-1832

Sales and Marketing Executives International
5500 Interstate North Parkway, 545
Atlanta, GA 30328
Website: www.smei.org

For information on trade show planning, write:

Trade Show Exhibitors Association
5501 Backlick Road, Suite 105
Springfield, VA 22151

Those interested in direct marketing can write:

American Teleservices Association
1620 One Street NW, Suite 615
Washington, DC 20006
Website: www.ataconnect.org

Direct Marketing Association
1120 Avenue of the Americas
New York, NY 10036-6700
Website: www.the-dma.org

Direct Selling Association
1666 K Street NW, Suite 1010
Washington, DC 20006-2808
Website: www.dsa.org

Women in Direct Marketing International
224 7th Street
Garden City, NY 11530
Website: www.wdmi.org

1. Honeycutt, Earl D., et al. "Student Preferences for Sales Careers Around the Pacific Rim," *Industrial Marketing Management* 28 (January 1999).
2. Luthy, Michael R. "Preparing the Next Generation of Industrial Sales Representatives." *Industrial Marketing Management* 29 (May 2000).
3. Steele, Georgia. "Predicting New Leads." *Business and Management Practices* 2 (February 2000): 30.
4. Littman, Margaret. "Busy as a B2B: As Internet Shifts to Heavy Industry, Chicago Buzzes with New Ventures." *Crain's Chicago Business*, March 13, 2000, 17.
5. Blackmon, Douglas A. "Price Buster." *The Wall Street Journal*, July 17, 2000, R12.
6. "iSwag.com Announces DUO Version 1.0." *Business Wire*, May 18, 2000.
7. "Marketing Database Associates, Inc. Launches mda-energyleads.com to Provide Sales Lead Distribution Solution for Utilities & Energy Service Providers." *Business Wire*, March 6, 2000.
8. Davidson, Paul. "Manufacturers Squeeze the Hands That Sell Them." *USA Today*, June 4, 1999, 1B.
9. DiSabatino, Jennifer. "GM Considers Online Sales Site for All Makes." *Computerworld*, February 12, 2001, 24.
10. Webb, Dave. "Making the Most of Image." *Canadian Business and Current Affairs* 2 (February 2000): 15.
11. "Nonstore (Catalog) Retailing Performance." *Business and Industry, Chain Store Age State of the Industry Supplement*, August 2000, 14A.
12. Jerry, Markon. "'Don't-Call' Laws Raise False Hope for Peace, Quiet." *The Wall Street Journal*, Friday, December 22, 2000, B1.

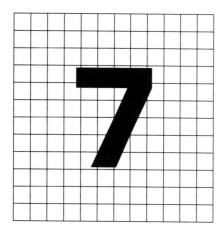

CAREERS IN RETAILING

Retailing has a vital role in driving the economy. Retailers must respond to economic ups and downs and factors that affect consumer shopping patterns such as dual-income families, a higher birthrate, time pressures, changes in lifestyle, more choices in products, and easier access to information. These factors have contributed to growth in the use of non-store shopping including home shopping television networks, catalog retailers, and the Internet. Today, retailers cannot focus all of their resources on in-store shopping but must figure out how to allocate these resources on selling opportunities outside the store to meet customer needs and keep them satisfied.[1] Generation Y, teens between the ages of 12 and 19, is estimated to grow to its largest number in U.S. history—35 million by 2010. Retailers are appealing to this huge market, $153 billion in 1999, with magazine/catalog hybrids called "magalogs" that link products and stories, free CDs and music, and contests.[2] Another huge market has the attention of retailers—78 million baby boomers with roughly 36 million children between the ages of 4 and 12 spend or influence more than $550 billion in annual sales. The market for products for juveniles is nearly $5 billion.[3] Retailers that have become more family-friendly include Starbucks, which has added play areas to many of its stores, Home Depot, which offers weekly workshops for kids, and Barnes & Noble, which added kids' menus and CD listening stations.[4] Retailing is a combination of activities involved in selling goods and services directly to consumers for personal or household use. The activities of retail establishments include buying items from manufacturers and wholesalers, advertising, accounting, data processing, materials management, and personal selling, the latter being the key to successful retailing. Retail establishments come in all sizes from large department stores to the tiny shop on the corner with one employee—the owner. Figure 7.1 shows different types of retail stores.

This chapter focuses on in-store retailing. Chapter 6 discussed non-store retailing. Retail professions fall into basically two groups: those involved in purchasing the goods offered for sale in retail stores, including merchandise man-

Figure 7.1 Types of Retail Stores

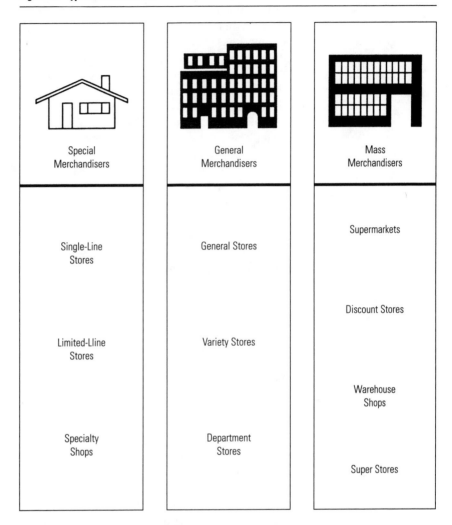

Special Merchandisers	General Merchandisers	Mass Merchandisers
Single-Line Stores	General Stores	Supermarkets
		Discount Stores
Limited-Lline Stores	Variety Stores	Warehouse Shops
Specialty Shops	Department Stores	Super Stores

agers, buyers, and assistant buyers; and those involved in selling goods to the public, including department managers and salespeople. This chapter explores these and other retail professions.

TRENDS IN RETAILING

The late 1990s were a bonanza for retailers with an average annual growth rate of 6.5 percent, as affluent shoppers enjoyed spending their stock market gains. Productivity grew by 5.1 percent with roughly 12.5 million employed in retailing by 2000.[5] In that same year, Americans owed $650 billion on their credit cards, an increase of 10 percent over 1999, while after-tax income increased only half as much.[6] Past spending by consumers, an uncertain economic outlook, rising energy prices, and other economic factors all affect retail sales. Consumers have become more price conscious, and discount stores like Target and Kohl's and online retailers pull customers from the higher end stores. Retailers who counted on a continuing economic boom and expanded too rapidly are facing store closings and mergers, while all retailers will have to concentrate on maintaining their existing markets.

Retailers have begun to expand their holdings into Canada over the past decade. The number of Wal-Marts has increased; Home Depot has entered Canada; Staples acquired the Business Depot chain and is beating out its rivals; Gap doubled the number of Canada stores; and Price/Costco expanded its number of stores. Wal-Mart has expanded rapidly in Mexico. The challenge to retailers in the future will be to avoid high levels of debt, target specific markets, and use technology to reduce cost and improve service. Panelists at a recent retail trends conference in Toronto, where small independent retailers have a larger sales volume than large department stores, discussed the importance of adding main-street types of entertainment to the malls to appeal to the younger consumers.[7]

Along with discount stores, warehouse clubs, and outlet malls, price-conscious consumers are looking for bargains on the Internet and in used merchandise establishments. Recycling as a retail trend is evident in the growth of used-merchandise stores such as Grow Biz International, Play It Again Sports, and Once Upon a Child. These stores do not have a Goodwill or pawn shop atmosphere, but feel and operate like any other retail establishment.

Specialty Stores

The 1980s saw the rise in popularity of the specialty store. This change in the shopping habits of the American public has been attributed to the needs of the increasing number of working women. Such specialty stores as apparel stores, bookstores, toy stores, sporting goods stores, and others offer a narrow product line but a deep range within the line. They stock more styles, colors, sizes, or models with varying features, giving the shopper more choices. Shopping is less complicated and time-consuming because there are no long lines or confusing departments. Specialty stores are handy for lunch-hour shopping or quick stops after work. If a specific item is unavailable, shop owners are usually willing to order it and call the customer when it arrives. More businesses keep popping up to fill the new strip shopping centers—more convenient than large shopping malls. New businesses will be discussed in Chapter 10 in the section on entrepreneurship.

Variety Stores

General merchandise stores such as department stores and variety stores have undergone some dramatic changes over the years. Bloomingdale's, Macy's, Saks

Fifth Avenue, Dillard's, and other department stores around the country are synonymous with style. Although these stores have numerous departments, including toys, furniture, sporting goods, books, and home decorations, their real strength is clothing. In order to compete with discount and specialty stores, department stores have both budget shops and designer departments. For those in fashion-related merchandising and sales, the greater emphasis on clothing is good news. Sometimes in the fashion industry values clash. In a recent court case, Calvin Klein sued his partner company Warnaco, which produces his line of blue jeans, charging that his high prestige jeans are being sold in discount stores and the style and quality of his jeans is being altered.[8] The suit was eventually settled amicably.

The 1950s through the 1970s saw the development of suburban shopping centers and the deterioration of downtown shopping. However, throughout the 1980s downtown shopping malls began to develop again. These malls contain fashionable department stores, specialty shops, and restaurants that cater to tourists, conventioneers, and lunch-hour shoppers in the downtown area.

Retailers must constantly adapt to changes in consumer shopping patterns. Woolworth's changed from a variety to a specialty merchant. Closing many of its variety stores (former five-and-dimes), Woolworth's opened eleven hundred new brand stores in 1988, including Champs, Kids Mart, Herald Square, and Lady Foot Locker. Walgreen Company, on the other hand, started to sell beer, wine, soda, snacks, milk, bread, and frozen TV dinners along with the usual drugstore merchandise. Though prescription and nonprescription drugs are the fastest growing portion of Walgreen's business and likely to remain so as the population ages, this convenience-store approach has worked well.

Discount Stores

Mass merchandising retailers offer a wide variety of products usually at discount prices in large, self-service stores. Opportunities in sales are greatly reduced, purchasing is centralized, and services are nearly nonexistent. However, management opportunities exist in these stores, and many chains are experiencing phenomenal growth. Discount stores, super stores, warehouse clubs, and warehouse and catalog showrooms are examples of mass merchandising retailers.

Factory outlet malls increased in number over the 1990s. Initially these outlet malls contained only manufacturers' shops, and some contained only upscale manufacturers. Now, outlet malls are renting space to discount houses as well. Though the trend toward factory outlet shops and discount malls is likely to continue, the numbers of new malls alone suggest that there will be more competition and some failures.

Wal-Mart, needing new avenues of growth, acquired Wholesale Club and Pace to increase its share of the warehouse club business. Sam's and Price/Costco now share a large percentage of the warehouse club market. Specialty retailers such as Home Depot, Office Depot, The Sports Authority, and PetSmart have imitated the format of the large variety wholesale clubs. A widening gap between rich and poor is attributed to numerous factors, including declines in the manufacturing segment of the economy, a lessening union influence to keep salaries up, and stiffer educational requirements for better-paying jobs. Because of this shift, retailers have begun to cater more to low-income shoppers. The future looks promising for discount stores and warehouse clubs.

ADVANCED TECHNOLOGY AND E-COMMERCE

Retailing today is placing greater emphasis on technology and professional management. Supermarkets and large discount stores have used computerized cash registers and point-of-sale terminals for years. Up-to-the-minute sales information is available to more and more retailers. Executives with both merchandising and management skills who can increase profits and worker productivity through use of the new technology will be in demand. Large discount retailers exact careful control over their inventory by tying into their suppliers electronically. Electronic inter-company inventory management enables retailers and their suppliers to maintain inventory as needed and will change the way buyers work.

The National Retail Federation/Forrester Online Retail Index provides information to retailers compiled from monthly surveys of 5,000 online shoppers detailing how much money is spent online and on what products.[9] Also involved is Greenfield Online, a major Internet-enabled consumer research data provider. In a separate survey conducted by Greenfield Online, results showed that Americans who use the Internet command 60 percent of the buying power of the total U.S. population. The survey revealed books to be the big online customer winner since half of Internet users buy their books online. Though most people still purchase software at local stores, more consumers buy software over the Internet than at malls or from catalogs. Malls and local stores still dominate apparel purchases, with 68 percent and 66 percent respectively, but online apparel purchases, which are at 18 percent, are nearly as popular as catalog purchases at 22 percent.[10]

Retailers are using websites to sell merchandise online and deliver it to customers from local distribution centers. Staples Inc., which generates $9 billion annually from office supplies, has created a site that includes options to simplify selection from its many products and get feedback from customers.[11] However, Staples.com estimated a loss of $250 million on sales of $150 million in 2000.[12] With all of the Internet hype and new E-businesses, it is JC Penney who is the largest online retailer of apparel and home furnishings, according to Nielsen/Net Ratings, with 1.3 million visitors a month to its website, 18 percent of which make purchases generating an estimated $303 million in sales in 2000.[13] Instead of suffering from online competition, Penney's has managed to dominate, even as sales in its stores are sagging.

Many unique challenges exist for new Internet retailers and for established retailers trying to maintain their market share by tapping into the online bonanza. Numerous online companies have gone under with the slowdown of the economy. Funding has dried up, consumers aren't buying, and entrepreneurs have realized that they need to know a lot more about business. Online shoppers still have numerous concerns about shipping charges, inability to judge the quality and fit of many items, return policies, credit card safety, delivery times, and the inability to ask questions about products.[14] Still, growth in Internet purchases suggests that convenience, timesaving, and technology have great appeal in today's culture.

RETAIL SALES

Customer service is the key to successful retail sales. A recent American Express survey revealed some differences in how customers of different ages value service, finding that the majority of shoppers over 55 prefer personal attention from salespeople, those between 35 and 55 want an easy return/exchange program, and shoppers under 35 want fast checkout service.[15] Successful retail salespeople understand the preferences of different customers, know their store's merchandise, and are very effective in dealing with the public. Customers come into retail establishments to purchase specific items, comparison shop, or merely to browse. The people who deal directly with these customers can make or break a business. An ability to communicate well, a courteous manner, and a positive attitude are three prerequisites for success in selling any product. Many people reject the idea of a career in sales because they dislike the hard sell. It also repels customers. The successful salesperson finds out what customers want and need, determines what merchandise meets this need, persuades the customer to buy it, and makes the customer feel good about the purchase. Essentially, the best selling is actually helping the customer buy. Customer service is the real key to successful selling.

Mass merchandising. The most basic type of sales and customer service occurs in mass merchandising, where customer inquiries usually have to do with whether the store stocks an item and where it can be found. Knowledge of store layout and merchandise is necessary. Although these positions do not involve commissions and do involve stocking shelves more than actual selling, they provide good full-time and part-time jobs for those with little formal education and for students. They also offer experience that other employers often seek and can lead to supervisory positions in sales.

Specialty sales. Sales work in fashion apparel, cosmetics, and numerous other product lines requires greater product knowledge and sometimes requires special skills. For example, cosmetics salespeople sometimes give demonstrations as part of their sales presentation. Whether employed in a department of a large store or a small specialty shop, good salespeople must demonstrate friendly interest in their customers, a willingness to help, and considerable diplomacy.

Some clothes do not look good on some figures. Rather than selling a customer something that isn't flattering (a realization that the customer will reach sooner or later), a good salesperson will tactfully show the customer something that looks better. Helping customers involves much more than ringing up sales.

Commission sales. In selling expensive products such as cars, computers, and appliances, salespeople must not only know the capabilities of their products, they must also know why their products are superior to those of the competitors. Therefore, they need to be familiar with the competing products. Salespeople working on commission can have a large income if they generate many sales.

The retail sales professional. To be effective, sales professionals should:

1. Ascertain the wants and needs of customers.

2. Be familiar with the market and competition.

3. Understand and describe product features and uses.

4. Be able to explain the benefits to customers.

5. Learn effective selling techniques.

6. Know the importance of customer service.

7. Develop a positive attitude toward work.

Although customers come to the store, a salesperson needs both initiative and a customer service orientation to close more sales. Too often in large department stores the customer must seek out the salesperson. The salesperson with the initiative to approach the customer is far more likely to make the sale.

In retailing, it is important to understand the customer. For example, Brooks Brothers has catered to generations of men desiring traditional men's tailoring. When Marks & Spencer acquired Brooks Brothers, they shocked many loyal customers by installing escalators in 1989 and putting shirts and sweaters on open tables rather than in glass cases. These "innovations" along with jazzy new ads to attract younger clientele brought a host of complaints from regular customers. Every successful retail establishment has a solid customer base. Understanding the likes and dislikes of the store's customers and keeping them happy while luring new customers is important to sales personnel and management.

Whether selling goods or services, the selling professional must be reliable and responsive. The customer may not always be easy to deal with. Selling requires self-control and diplomacy. Everyone does not have the temperament for selling to the public, but for those who do, sales can be a lucrative and rewarding profession. Although sales positions offer the greatest number of job opportunities within retailing, there are other career options for individuals from a variety of educational backgrounds.

SALES MANAGEMENT

Sales management trainees may be recruited from the sales staff or from the pool of recent college graduates. MBAs have no real advantage in landing beginning retail management positions, though if hired they may earn slightly higher salaries. In retailing, hands-on experience is the real key. Compared to other marketing careers, experience is fairly easy to obtain by working in a part-time retail sales position while in college. Though often minimum-wage jobs, these part-time positions provide the necessary experience to land a good job after graduation. Large department stores actively recruit on college campuses, providing an excellent way for prospective graduates to make an initial contact. Applicants should ask about the company's management training program. Most large companies offer them.

Beginning as a department manager trainee, novices work with experienced managers throughout the store to observe all aspects of store operations. Under supervision, trainees handle staff scheduling, customer complaints, and record keeping. Once a trainee has demonstrated the ability to effectively supervise staff, work well with customers, and make good, quick decisions balancing the welfare of the store and the customer, the individual is promoted to manager of a small department.

The next level of promotion is usually to a larger department where the manager supervises more staff, handles more merchandise, and manages a larger budget in accordance with store policies. Such duties as scheduling workers, handling customer service requests and complaints, and monitoring how well merchandise is selling are all part of the job. Sales staff development is also important because, when promoted, effective department managers have already trained their replacements. Retail sales managers are usually given broad goals containing sales and profit expectations. How to reach or exceed these goals is up to the manager. Managers of exceptionally profitable departments are likely to be promoted to group sales manager. Directing several department managers and coordinating a sizable portion of store operations effectively may qualify an individual for assistant store manager, then store manager. The best retail store managers are selected for top corporate positions. Upwardly mobile managers are often targeted early in their careers and may be required to relocate every few years.

MERCHANDISE BUYING AND MANAGEMENT

Merchandising is a crucial part of the retail trade. Buyers purchase the merchandise that the store will sell. They decide what products will be offered for sale, arrange purchases from manufacturers, and set retail prices. Decisions are based on knowledge of customer tastes, changing trends, and a balance of quality and affordability. To make these decisions, buyers study marketing research reports, industry and trade publications, and the direction of the economy. It is speculated that Nordstrom's sales have not grown as anticipated since 1998 because women today want more casual clothes instead of the elegant designer fashions that have been Nordstrom's specialty in the past. This has resulted in increased markdowns of slow-selling items.[16] The workplace, cultural events such as theater, restaurants, and family social outings have all become more casual. It is important for those in fashion merchandising to keep pace with broad trends.

Because of the responsibility involved in spending large amounts of the store's money, the training period for buyers can range from two to five years. The entry-level merchandising position for college graduates is assistant buyer. After some store training, usually in sales, an assistant buyer works under a merchandising supervisor. Duties usually include speaking with manufacturers and placing approved orders for merchandise, inspecting new merchandise, and supervising its distribution throughout the department. During the first two to five years in buying, the novice becomes acquainted with manufacturers' lines, the store's needs, and the competition and begins to recommend products for purchase. Once promoted to buyer, duties expand to analyzing customer needs and choosing products to meet them. The role of the buyer is critical to the success of any retail establishment. For example, The Gap decreased its in-store basics, denim and T-shirts, to add new items such as flowing skirts, embroidered tops, and accessories. Cutting down on the number of basic items puts more pressure on the buyer to choose the right merchandise mix. Buyers normally begin in small departments and are promoted to larger departments.

The most promising buyers become merchandise managers whose primary duties are to supervise buyers. They oversee the department's budget, deciding how money should be divided among the buyers. Merchandise managers have a great impact on their store's image, its product offerings, and the direction of styles. They must develop a mix of brands to generate the most sales and profits, taking care to keep store brands from overwhelming other brands. Distribution managers oversee the movement of merchandise. They are responsible for receipt, ticketing, storage, and distribution of a store's inventory. The growing problem of customer and employee theft has resulted in a new management position—loss-prevention manager, whose duties include tracking inventory, price overrides, refunds, and employee purchases by using computers. Point-of-sale and electronic article surveillance systems are also used for security in theft-plagued retail outlets. Buyers who have been promoted through various management levels often reach the position of corporate merchandise manager. In this position, they may approve buying decisions for several stores in one state or in an entire region.

The bread and butter of large department stores is apparel. To fill the specialized position of fashion coordinator, an individual needs a background in fashion design, a portfolio to show artistic talent, a keen sense of style, good taste, and an awareness of sound business practice. Some large department stores employ fashion coordinators to work with buyers in selecting merchandise. Although glamorous work in that it may involve overseas buying, the position of fashion coordinator is not a step up the corporate ladder. It does, however, afford those with backgrounds in art or fashion merchandising an exciting and satisfying outlet for their artistic talents.

Another position requiring an art background is display designer. Large retailers design window and interior displays to promote sales. Recent graduates begin as apprentices and are trained on the job. Competition is very stiff for positions in fashion coordination and display as opportunities are very limited.

OPPORTUNITIES IN RETAILING

A tight labor market and a high turnover rate in sales positions puts pressure on retailers to find workers for entry-level sales positions. In Chicago, the Retail and Education Alliance for Development of Youth (READY) program helps fill this need by training and placing hundreds of high school students into summer retailing jobs.[17] Monster.com, the leading online careers site, recently launched Monster Retail, which links retail professionals with over 34,000 job postings.[18]

Retailing will continue to employ huge numbers of sales representatives. According to Occupational Employment Statistics (OES) survey data, there will be 1,938,000 new openings for retail salespersons, including store salespeople, between 1998 and 2008. About 66.5 percent of retail and personal services sales workers are self-employed. According to EUREKA 2000–2001, average pay for retail salespersons in 1998 was $1,580 per month. Between 1998 and 2008, 601,000 new jobs will be created for marketing and sales supervisors including retail store managers. First line supervisors earned $2,999 per month on average in 1998, while general managers and top executives averaged $5,214 per month. Factors such as level of responsibility and size of store affect salaries. Wholesale and retail buyers are projected to find 29,000 new openings between 1998 and 2008. Average pay in 1998 was $3,000 per month.

SOURCES OF INFORMATION

Staying up-to-date on trends is essential to retail professionals, especially buyers and merchandise and department managers. Such periodicals as *Advertising Age*, *Chain Store Age Executive*, *Discount Store News*, *The Fashion Newsletter*, *Inside Retailing Newsletter*, *Journal of Retailing*, *Stores*, and *Women's Wear Daily* are available in most public and college libraries to those interested in retail careers. Directories of retailers can be found in the reference section of the library, including *Fairchild's Financial Manual of Retail Stores*, *Nationwide Directory—Mass Market Merchandisers*, and *Sheldon's Retail Directory of the U.S. and Canada*.

As in other fields, retailing associations are another excellent source of inside information. Some are listed below.

American Marketing Association
311 South Wacker Drive, Suite 5800
Chicago, IL 60606
Website: www.ama.org

National Retail Federation
325 7th Street NW, Suite 1100
Washington, DC 20004
Website: www.nrf.com

General Merchandise Distributors Council
1275 Lake Plaza Drive, Suite C
Colorado Springs, CO 80906

International Mass Retail Association
1700 North Moore Street, Suite 2250
Arlington, VA 22209
Website: wwwimra.org

Sales and Marketing Executives International
5500 Interstate North Parkway, Number 545
Atlanta, GA 30328
Website: www.smei.org

Women in Sales Association
Eight Madison Avenue
P.O. Box M
Valhalla, NY 10595

1. Wellen, Jeffrey. "The Devotion Cycle: A Model for Helping Retailers Profit from Changing Consumer Values." *Chain Store Age Executive* 75: 52–54, 67.
2. Barrett, Amy. "To Reach the Unreachable Teen." *Business Week*, September 18, 2000, 78–80.
3. Reidy, Chris. "Demographic, Retail Trends Help Canton, Mass., Safety-Products Maker." *Boston Globe*, February 10, 2000.
4. Horovitz, Bruce. "Targeting the Kindermarket: Family-Friendly Retailers Try to Attract Parents, Build Loyalty." *USA Today*, March 3, 2000, 1B.
5. Pascual, Alex M. "Retail." *Business Week*, January 8, 2001, 128.
6. DeGross, Renee. "Retailers' Hopes for Big Holiday Wane." *The Atlanta Journal and Constitution*, December 19, 2000.
7. "Main-Streeting the Malls." *Canadian Business and Current Affairs* 49, no. 2 (May 1999): 21.
8. Sellers, Patricia. "Seventh Avenue Smackdown." *Fortune*, September 4, 2000, 223–232.
9. "National Retail Federation and Forrester Research Announce Online Retail Index." *Business Wire*, January 17, 2000.

10. "Internet Sales Eating Away at Bricks & Mortar Retailing." *PR Newswire*, March 22, 1999.
11. Schwartz, Mathew. "Sharper Staples." *Computerworld*, June 12, 2000, 76–78.
12. Bulkeley, William M. "Clicks and Mortar." *The Wall Street Journal*, July 17, 2000, R4.
13. Kelly, Barron. "Penney Wise." *Forbes*, September 4, 2000, 72.
14. Quick, Rebecca. "Returns to Sender." *The Wall Street Journal*, July 17, 2000, R8.
15. "Older and Younger Shoppers Differ Dramatically Regarding Importance of Customer Service Attributes, Found an American Express Survey." *PR Newswire*, April 6, 1999.
16. Much, Marilyn. "Nordstrom Looks at Family Values as Answer to Sales, Earnings Skid." *Investor's Business Daily*, November 22, 2000, A1.
17. Baeb, Eddie. "Program Gets Teens Ready for Retail Jobs: Needs Merchant Funding to Help Expansion Effort." *Crain's Chicago Business*, October 4, 1999, 25.
18. "Monster.com Launches Targeted Career Community for Retail Professionals, Just in Time for Holiday Season" *Business Wire*, October 16, 2000.

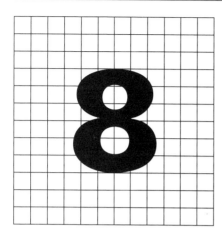

CAREERS IN MARKETING MANAGEMENT

Promotion to a top corporate marketing position may occur from within company ranks, but not always. In 1999, J.C. Penney Co. broke with its tradition and hired outsider Stephen Farley as senior vice president and chief marketing officer from Payless Shoesource Inc. Having held senior marketing jobs with Pizza Hut and Earl Palmer Brown Inc., and prior to that having worked at advertising agencies N.W. Ayer and Saatchi and Saatchi Inc., he brought new experience to the company that helped regain Penney's lost market share and attracted younger shoppers. At the same time however, two Penney's veterans were also promoted—Marilee J. Cumming to president of merchandising for J.C. Penney stores and catalog and Michael W. Taxter to senior vice president and director of J.C. Penney stores.[1]

No matter how high in the company a manager rises, he or she never stops selling. Billionaire investor Warren Buffett accepted an invitation in early 1993 to speak to the directors and top executives of General Motors. Jack Smith, GM's CEO, found out that Buffett didn't drive a GM car. Buffett explained that he switched from Cadillacs to a Lincoln Town Car because it had dual airbags. In February of 1994, Buffett received a note from Smith informing him that Cadillac was now equipped with airbags that not only handled the driver and the passenger in the end seat but also the passenger sitting in the middle. Buffett was so impressed with Smith's memory and dogged salesmanship that he promised to buy a Cadillac the next time he purchased a car.

Throughout the functional areas of corporate marketing—marketing research, product development, advertising, sales promotion, public relations, and sales—outstanding individuals advance to management levels. The top position is vice-president of marketing, who has authority over all marketing activities in a corporation. Often a marketing vice-president will advance to the position of chief executive officer (CEO). Figure 8.1 is a corporate organization chart showing chain of command and levels of authority. This hierarchy

Figure 8.1 Top and Middle Levels of Corporate Marketing Management

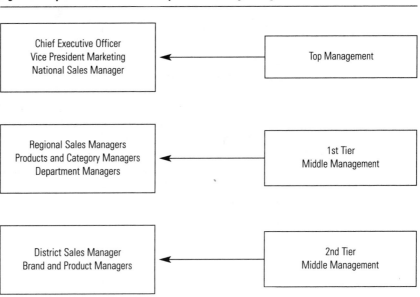

varies from firm to firm depending on the number of levels of management and how marketing functions are organized within the firm.

Corporations have streamlined management considerably. In the 1970s it was customary to have as many as twelve to fifteen levels of supervision in large corporations. Today the norm is five or six levels. This is the result of major restructuring brought about by a wave of acquisitions and divestitures, increased global competition, an attempt at creating a more entrepreneurial environment to foster new product development, and fluctuations in the economy. The reduction of middle-level managers has increased both the complexity and the pressures of management positions.

THE RESTRUCTURING OF CORPORATE MANAGEMENT

The past two decades were characterized by thousands of mergers, acquisitions, and divestitures. As companies and pieces of companies were bought and sold, hundreds of thousands of managers and professionals were forced to change jobs or retire early. In many cases, middle-level management positions were never refilled. Major reorganizations took place in companies. Top management realized that if the firm was to compete in a more competitive, rapidly changing business environment, it had to respond more rapidly to change. Improved productivity and a leaner corporate structure enabled managers to introduce products into the market more efficiently.

For years, small companies have received the most credit for introducing new technology into the marketplace. One of the reasons for this is the efficiency of a less-formal corporate structure. In large companies various levels of management review new product development plans; small companies, functioning as entrepreneurial teams, are able to move a product rapidly from the drawing board to the marketplace. The message is clear—until large corporations become more entrepreneurial both in philosophy and in practice, they will be unable to beat their small competitors into the marketplace with new products.

Big companies responded to the challenge by creating more project or product development teams. These teams were given the authority to operate fairly autonomously both in fulfilling goals and competing for company resources, as was described in Chapter 3. Product managers reported directly to marketing managers at top levels in the company. Because the teams were entrepreneurial in spirit, yet part of a large corporation, the term "intrepreneuring" was coined.

With fewer levels of management and tighter budgets, companies were unable to reward managers with promotions and raises as they once did. However, fewer job titles and pay grades make it easier to base raises on performance rather than seniority. One way companies motivate promising young managers is with a lateral or sideways move that offers a new challenge and enables young managers to learn another part of the company's operations. Giving more responsibility and autonomy to subordinates is another way to keep young managers from getting bored. Overseas assignments for managers are inevitable as companies expand their global operations. At companies where a large percentage of sales are foreign, an overseas assignment is necessary for promotion to top management. Finally, more companies are offering up-and-coming executives mid-career breaks by sending them to management development programs designed by business schools especially for executives.

MARKETING MANAGERS

Top-level executives determine an organization's mission and make policy. The executive vice-president for marketing directs overall marketing policy, the effect of which is felt at every level and function of the marketing process. The marketing management concept permeating the field today is broader in scope because of the increasingly complex business and economic environment in which the firms of today must operate. Top-level production and finance managers must be convinced that marketing policies will enable the firm to meet its overall goals and objectives. The top marketing executive spends considerable time selling these policies to the CEO and other top officers.

All marketing managers are involved in planning, implementing, and controlling marketing activities and decisions. These functions are common to all managers, but marketing managers at the top of the organization are primarily involved in planning. Planning includes setting objectives and standards of performance and developing strategies and tactics to implement those objectives. Marketing strategy addresses such issues as what markets to enter, what products to offer, how to allocate marketing resources, and, for large corporations, what companies to buy. Marketing executives must make such global decisions in consultation with finance, production, and sales executives. Objectives and strategies are communicated to lower level marketing managers who then develop the detailed marketing strategy required to implement the plans.

MIDDLE MANAGERS AND SUPERVISORS

Implementation involves organizing, staffing, directing, and coordinating the organization's resources. All marketing managers are involved in implementation activities to some extent. But unlike top managers, who spend most of their time in strategic planning, middle-level managers such as department heads and project team leaders are primarily involved in implementation. Hiring staff, assigning duties, directing and overseeing projects, distributing the budget throughout the department, and other such activities are the responsibility of department heads.

Middle-level managers and supervisors are responsible for measuring staff performance to see that objectives are met and taking corrective action if they are not. Specific objectives related to deadlines for projects, planned budgets, and sales quotas are measurable. If objectives are not met, it is up to managers to determine whether they were unrealistic, or whether either external factors or worker performance is responsible. Corrective action may involve revising objectives, making adjustments to allow for external factors, or working with staff to solve problems.

The work of middle managers and supervisors has been discussed throughout the chapters of this book. They manage staffs of professionals and technicians working in the various activities of marketing. Managers of marketing research, product development, advertising, sales promotion, public relations, and regional sales all report to top-level marketing managers. In the absence of many levels of middle managers, these managers operate their departments more autonomously and have more authority over both activities and budgets. Their offices are usually located close to top management, and communications are considerably less formal than in the huge bureaucracies of the past. Though chain of command is still intact in many organizations where managers at every level formally report to a designated individual, communications are considerably more relaxed and pragmatic in most organizations.

Technology has changed corporate communications forever. Each manager has a personal computer usually hooked into a central computer through local area network (LAN) technology. Branch computers are hooked into the central computer through wide area network (WAN) technology. Thus, improved communications technology has enabled the free flow of information throughout the organization. Management information systems (MIS) and decision support systems (DSS) provide a systematic way of disseminating information needed for management decisions. A system is a collection of people, machines, programs, and procedures organized to perform a certain task. Marketing information systems provide marketing managers a steady flow of timely, accurate information from a variety of sources both inside and outside the organization that they can then use to make decisions. Computers and communications technology have reduced the need for managers whose main job was organizing and communicating this type of information.

SUCCEEDING IN MANAGEMENT

A top-level manager's background doesn't necessarily assure success within a specific corporate setting. For this reason, many companies such as Bristol-Myers Squibb, Dell Computer, General Electric, and Motorola are using psychological evaluations costing around $5,000 to determine whether executive candidates will fit well into the corporate culture.[2] Despite an individual's qualifications and talent, succeeding within a unique culture often depends on specific values and personality traits. Marketing professionals should carefully choose a company, find a mentor, and use whatever resources are available. Choosing and being chosen by the right company is a complicated issue. Company offers to new college graduates may be evaluated in terms of salary, benefits, and growth potential. Chapters 11 and 12 address many issues that will help graduates evaluate the job market and company offers that they will receive. But very little of the internal working of the company can be gleaned from company literature or job interviews. Only when working for a company can an individual learn the intricacies of how decisions are made and where the power resides.

ATTRACTING A MENTOR

The single most important action that a new employee takes is finding a mentor. A mentor is an older professional in the same field, preferably making steady career progress within the company. Good mentors offer introductions to people higher up and a good many insights into the unspoken rules of the company. Every company has a unique corporate culture and its own way of doing things. Finding a mentor is not easy. Any mentor worth having is extremely busy and not out looking for proteges. The young employee who shows persistence yet flexibility, works hard to obtain recognition, listens to everything going on in the company before taking strong positions or forming alliances, has clearly stated career goals, and displays confidence and pride as well as ability will attract attention before long. Many employees have followed their mentors right up the hierarchy by filling the positions they vacate on the way up.

WOMEN IN MANAGEMENT

Women are rising to key marketing positions in companies. With extensive experience in brand management, Fiona Dias became vice president of marketing for the Frito-Lay Division of PepsiCo, Inc., then chief marketing officer of Stick Networks, a new company producing Internet appliances, and today holds the position of senior vice president of marketing for Circuit City Stores, Inc.[3] Despite the success of women like Nina E. McLemore, founder of Liz Claiborne Accessories and current president of Regent Capital Management, women hold only 7 percent of the managerial positions having profit-and-loss responsibility, according to a 2000 Catalyst study.[4] These are the types of positions that lead to top management. Women now hold 22 percent of all managerial positions, a gain of 14 percent since 1990, but occupy less than 10 percent of the seats on corporate boards, as cited in the 2000 National Management Salary Survey conducted by the Institute of Management and Remuneration Economics.[5] This is despite a growing body of comprehensive management studies showing women executives are rated higher by bosses, peers, and subordinates than their male counterparts in a wide variety of areas including producing high quality work, goal-setting, and mentoring. However, a study showed that male CEOs and senior vice-presidents got high ratings if they were forceful and assertive and lower if they were cooperative and empathic, while female CEOs got lower ratings for being assertive and higher when they were cooperative.[6] Perceptions change slowly at the top of the corporation.

It is particularly important for women to have mentors because females are greatly underrepresented in top levels of management in larger companies. Women's salaries lag behind those of men for the same positions. Women in management in large corporations often identify "a male-dominated corporate culture" as an obstacle to success. Some companies, however, make a concerted effort to remove obstacles to women's advancement into corporate management ranks through programs such as awareness training for men. Some companies even set goals for promoting women.

Past studies have identified companies with woman-friendly corporate cultures. The factors considered were numbers of women in key executive positions and on the board of directors, specific efforts to help women advance, and sensitivity to the work/family dilemma. Companies such as Avon, CBS, Dayton-Hudson, Gannett, Kelly Services, U.S. West, American Express, Baxter International, Corning, Honeywell, IBM, Johnson & Johnson, Merck, Monsanto, Pitney Bowes, Reader's Digest, Security Pacific Bank, and Square D. have been acknowledged in these areas. These companies are in a wide variety of industries. Women have fared very well in computer companies, entering in substantial numbers when their skills were very much needed at the birth of the industry. But other industries represented in this group are old, conservative industries such as banking and electrical manufacturing. These companies reversed usual practices to become woman-friendly.

Though women have had to work hard to prove themselves, every successful woman changes a few minds. Women's networks in companies often help other women learn the ropes. It is important for young women aspiring to management positions to be aware of how women are faring at the companies making them offers. Questions to ask at interviews should be what percentage of women hold top management posts? Middle management posts? Do company benefits include extended leaves, flextime, and day-care assistance? The best offer for a new graduate may not come from a woman-friendly company but from a company offering excellent training and development opportunities. Trade-offs are always present in job offers. It is important for both men and women to carefully articulate their short- and long-range goals before entering the job market.

TOP CHIEF EXECUTIVE OFFICERS

The chief executive officers (CEOs) in large traditional U.S. companies have a number of attributes in common. Many come from wealthy families or those in which the heads of the households are corporate managers, successful professionals, or owners of medium-sized businesses. Many CEOs attended Ivy League schools such as Yale, Princeton, and Harvard. The next-largest group attended Big Ten schools. Some attended military schools. Almost all hold bachelor's degrees. Many have graduate degrees. Most CEOs are married with children. A large number enjoy sports, particularly golf and tennis.

CEOs have come up from a variety of functional areas including finance/accounting, merchandising/marketing, engineering/technical, production/manufacturing, and the legal department. Most CEOs have worked for more than one company. Movement from one company to another occurs as boards attempt to find executives to lead companies through restructuring. In general, CEOs are multitalented, versatile people. There is little room at the top, and most new graduates hardly expect to become CEOs of large corporations. Still, the backgrounds of CEOs give some hints about the types of people who have made it to the top in the past.

RESOURCES FOR MANAGERS

Three major areas of resources for professional managers are company training and continuing education, professional organizations, and marketing periodicals.

Management Training and Development

Management training and development is an important ingredient in the success formula for marketing professionals. Without good training and development opportunities, individuals can become stagnant early in their careers. The first question that a job applicant should ask is, "What kind of training and development will the company provide me if I accept this position?" To meet training needs, some companies are allowing employees to select the pace of training that takes place both inside and outside the work environment. This partnership enables ambitious employees to have more control over training opportunities and to advance at their own rate. In addition to the traditional stand-up lecture, company training programs employ technologies such as interactive video, computer-based training, television courses, and numerous others. *The National Directory of Corporate Training Programs* provides information on such training programs and the companies that offer them.

Formal training programs for managers and professionals are offered through business schools. Major restructuring in corporations has caused the emphasis of executive training to be placed on organizational transformation rather than personal development. Business schools are offering more custom programs designed for specific corporations. These programs, as well as in-house programs, are geared to meet specific goals or to transform corporate culture. In the past, General Electric Company sent managers to a program to learn how to develop markets in the fast-growing economies of Asia. Ford used management development to encourage closer cooperation across disciplines, that is, to create more product-oriented marketing people and vice versa. Cigna Corporation used team-building activities to tackle real company problems culminating in recommendations to senior management.

Going to work for a company that offers its employees training and development programs and support should be an important career objective. Continuing education programs offered through colleges and universities enable individuals to increase their chances of promotion. Many companies pay tuition costs for job-related courses, even entire MBA programs. An MBA is helpful, often necessary, to advance through management ranks. Professionals are responsible for their own training and career development regardless of the type of training and continuing education opportunities an employer provides. Training opportunities are also available to members through their professional organizations. By joining professional organizations as a student, one can take advantage of some early training opportunities and gain a competitive edge.

Professional Management Organizations

Participation in professional organizations is very beneficial to marketing professionals and students. The organizations provide an opportunity for communication among members at meetings and conferences. In addition, a tremendous amount of current information is disseminated through advanced training and seminars sponsored by the organizations. Many offer placement services for new college graduates. The price of membership for students is greatly reduced in most cases.

A good source for names and addresses of professional organizations is the *Encyclopedia of Associations*, which is published annually and can be found in the reference section of the library. Information includes names, addresses, and phone numbers of professional associations; the date they were founded; the number of current members; a description of the membership; and publications, if any. In addition to the organizations related to specific areas of marketing listed in the various chapters, many marketing managers hold memberships in the following associations:

American Management Association
1601 Broadway
New York, NY 10019-7420
Website: www.amanet.org

American Marketing Association
311 South Wacker Drive, Suite 5800
Chicago, IL 60606
Website: www.ama.org

Association of MBA Executives, Inc.
AMBA Center
5 Summit Place
Branford, CT 06405

National Association for Female Executives
135 W. 59th Street, 16th floor
New York, NY 10020
Website: www.nafe.com

Sales and Marketing Executives, International
5500 Interstate North Parkway, Number 545
Atlanta, GA 30328
Website: www.smei.org

Women in Management
920 South Spring Street
Springfield, IL 62704

Management Newsletters and Journals

Many professional associations publish newsletters and journals. Marketing periodicals are excellent sources of general information. An impressive list can be found in *Ulrich's International Periodicals Directory* in the reference section of the library. It is published annually by R.R. Bowker Company, New York and London. A good many marketing periodicals can be found in public and university libraries. Most marketing professionals subscribe to a number of periodicals to keep current and gain professional insights. Also included in many newsletters and journals are classified ads posting job openings. Many resources for managers are online.

OPPORTUNITIES FOR MANAGERS

The number of managerial jobs will rise 21 percent between 1998 and 2010, according to Development Dimensions International.[7] Management Recruiters International reports that much of this demand will be for sales and marketing managers, with nearly 60 percent of executives surveyed in 2000 planning to add positions.[8] Demand will vary considerably from industry to industry. Business and information services should experience strong growth along with advertising, sales promotion, and public relations agencies. Much of this growth in service agencies is due to outsourcing, a trend among companies toward contracting work to outside agencies, and is likely to continue. This growth will create many new opportunities for marketing managers. The restructuring going on in large corporations will create a demand for product and brand managers to head up teams.

Companies undergoing radical change are firing and retiring managers with old ideas and hiring others to help with the change process. Executive search firms report record amounts of billings for senior managers and the most active CEO market that they have ever seen. The greatest rise in demand is for marketing executives. Marketing executives are considered by some to be the only true generalists in the company because of their overall industry perspective. Consequently, they are in great demand even in technology-oriented companies and particularly in the telecommunications and software industries.

MANAGEMENT COMPENSATION

The federal government put a $1 million cap on corporate deductibility of executive salaries. The irony is that the law established a standard of sorts so that companies that used to pay less than $1 million have upped CEO salaries to that level. Others award higher salaries and suffer the tax consequences, or rather, the stockholders suffer the consequences. Executive compensation is now, however, undergoing some changes. Boards of directors are hiring pay consultants to help determine what their people are worth. A trend to link CEOs' paychecks to corporate performance has definitely taken hold.

Salary is not always the most significant part of the compensation package. Stock holdings in the company can amount to millions, sometimes billions. Consider the stock holdings of the following CEOs as of May 25, 2000:

Bill Gates, Microsoft	$48.3 billion
Jeffrey Besos, Amazon.com	$15.9 billion
Philip Knight, Nike	$4.1 billion
John Stanton, Western Wireless/ VoiceStream Wireless	$879.0 million

Barry Ackerly, The Ackerly Group	$240.5 million
Howard Schultz, Starbucks	$223.1 million
Edward Fritzky, Immunex	$210.5 million
Dennis Morrison, Morris Knudsen	$151.2 million
James Sinegal, Costco Wholesale	$145.9 million
Jeffrey Brotman, Costco Wholesale	$136.1 million

Although stock values vary with the market, these holdings are pretty impressive.[9]

Management compensation varies widely depending on the industry, level of management, size of budget, scope of responsibility, and expertise and reputation. CEOs of nonprofit organizations may earn lower pay. Though women executives in sales and management earn less than men, there is some indication that the base salary for women executives is increasing at a faster rate than that of men. Benefits such as stock options and long-term compensation vary greatly as well. Each management position and its compensation package must be evaluated individually. According to reported figures in EUREKA 2000–2001, base salaries in 1998 for entry-level managers with bachelor's degrees ranged from $2,000 to $5,000 per month. New graduates from MIT averaged $3,733 per month. Experienced managers earned from $2,300 to $6,934 per month; top pay ranged from $5,000 to $14,786. Most highly paid CEOs can make from $100,000 to $440,000 per month.

In Canada, stock options and other pay incentives are frequently used to reward executives in high performing companies. Executive Compensation Practices in the TSE 300, 2000, a survey of Canadian executives conducted by Watson Wyatt Worldwide, reported average total compensation for CEOs including incentive pay as $1.2 million with a base salary of $528,000. Average annual incentive pay for the top five executives exceeds 60 percent of base salary in high performing companies and may be as much as 100 percent for CEOs.[10] More relevant figures for the purposes of this book are the salaries of recent graduates, which are discussed in Chapter 11.

1. Halkais, Maria. "J.C. Penney Names Outsider to High-Level Post." *The Dallas Morning News*, June 2, 1999.
2. Daniels, Cora. "Does This Man Need a Shrink?" *Fortune*, February 5, 2001, 205.
3. "Circuit City Appoints Senior Vice President, Marketing." *PR Newswire*, November 27, 2000.
4. Gutner, Toddi. "She Did It By the Numbers." *Business Week*, December 11, 2000, 130.
5. Coleman, Alison. "Number of Women Executives Reaching Corporate Boardrooms Remains Low." *Daily Mail*, November 5, 2000.

6. Sharpe, Rochele. "As Leaders, Women Rule." *Business Week*, November 20, 2000, 75–84.

7. Dierdorff, Jack. "Brain Drain." *Business Week*, September 20, 1999, 114.

8. "Headhunter.net Tackles Sales & Marketing Shortage." *Business Wire*, October 11, 2000.

9. DeSilver, Drew. "Northwest CEO Salary Survey." *The Seattle Times*, June 11, 2000, D1.

10. "Pay for Performance Clearly at the Forefront." *Canada News Wire*, October 3, 2000.

CAREERS IN GLOBAL MARKETING

According to a May 2000 report from the U.S. Bureaus of Census and Economic Analysis, U.S. exports reached almost $1 trillion in 1999. From a business standpoint the world is becoming more connected through trade agreements, communications technology, and the Internet. More opportunities for marketing products globally exist than ever before. One approach that companies are using today in new product development is the assembling of geographically dispersed global teams whose members differ by culture and language. Technologies such as videoconferencing, audioconferencing, and E-mail enable team members to communicate with each other around the world.[1] The new millennium has witnessed the emergence of China as a global trading partner with preferred trading status. Direct foreign investment is on the rise with fast-growing western economies cashing in on opportunities in developing countries. Singapore, Mexico, Argentina, and Malaysia are major beneficiaries of an influx of foreign capital. Latin America comprises a market of over 480 million consumers and is expected to grow to 674 million by 2025, with 80 percent in urban areas.[2] However, the affluent market may only grow to 12 million households over the next twenty years and the gap between rich and poor is growing.[3] Global marketing is a complicated field requiring in-depth cultural and demographic knowledge of potential markets. Global marketing, also called international marketing, multinational marketing, and transnational marketing, describes the activities of organizations that engage in exchanges across national borders. Both business and nonbusiness organizations such as charities, religious organizations, and universities are involved in global marketing. Whether selling products, soliciting donations, or recruiting students, these organizations operate in a global environment that has its own rules and requirements. Business organizations, whether U.S. based or headquartered abroad, are attempting to tap into the unprecedented growth in global marketing.

THE IMPACT OF FOREIGN COMPETITION ON U.S. CORPORATIONS

Competition from European and Asian markets has forced U.S. companies to think globally and become importers instead of exporters. The 1992 economic integration of the European Community has removed many trade barriers from country to country. Many U.S. companies in Europe have taken advantage of this, including Ford Motor Company, Merck & Company, Coca-Cola Company, IBM, and Hewlett-Packard Company, all of which have had successful operations in Europe for years. In Japan, McDonald's Corporation, Disney Company, DuPont Company, and Amway have prospered. Toys 'R' Us has stores in Canada, Europe, Hong Kong, Singapore, and Japan. To be successful, retailers must have the kind of format, supplier relationships, and expertise to operate with success globally.

The General Agreement on Tariffs and Trade (GATT) has removed many trade barriers from foreign trade. As foreign economies mature, they create huge markets for construction equipment, telecommunications products, and a host of other goods and services. More corporations have built or bought factories in Eastern Europe. The attraction to Eastern Europe is based on its large consumer market and educated labor force. Closer to home, the passage of the North American Free Trade Agreement (NAFTA) wiped out trade barriers such as protective tariffs and moved to create a unified North American economy. While free trade agreements have both positive and negative economic aspects for countries involved, these agreements do change the nature of the global marketplace and create opportunities.

CONSUMER DEMAND AND ITS IMPACT ON GLOBAL MARKETING

The developed countries of the world offer markets for U.S. products, but they are not growing significantly. Consumers in these mature economies have already satisfied most of their material needs. However, 77 percent of our global population lives in developing countries. Hundreds of millions of consumers in Asia will enter or approach middle class within the next ten years. They will want to buy a lot of cars, computers, appliances, and televisions. Eastern Europe contains millions of consumers all needing clothes, appliances, and the most basic of items. In Latin America, an awareness of international brands exists, so the demand is there and the marketing will be easier. This is especially true of the young who watch MTV and sip Coke in great numbers. Cultural barriers may, however, affect the introduction of certain products. A product such as tampons used by 70 percent of women in the United States, Canada, and much of Europe is used by just 2 percent of women in Latin America. After numerous failures to successfully introduce the product, Procter & Gamble has taken an approach in Mexico in which representatives meet with groups of women in a home, explain the product, and give participants a free box. Local women are hired to make these presentations as well as conduct mini-sessions in stores.[4] Those interested in careers in global marketing should broaden their perspective to include preparation to enter these diverse growing markets. Business will follow demand and businesses produce jobs.

Creating brands is as important worldwide as it is in the United States. CommonHealth Global Services, the world's largest healthcare-communications resource, which has fifteen divisions worldwide and comprises 85 percent of the market, helps client pharmaceutical companies build health brands, particularly throughout the United States and Europe.[5] Barclays Global Investors, the world's largest money manager, hired as head of global marketing Canadian Kathy Taylor, who is committed to using worldwide media to establish Barclays as a brand with all the loyalty and name recognition of popular consumer products.[6]

HOW COMPANIES ARE INVOLVED IN FOREIGN MARKETS

Companies have several options for entering foreign markets, including foreign operations, joint ventures, exporting, and licensing. These options differ in the level of financial commitment and risk involved.

Foreign Operations and Joint Ventures

Multinational companies commit a great deal of resources to establishing operations in foreign countries, and they often take on a lot of risk. They run the risk of consumers rejecting their products, and they are also faced with political risks including confiscation of their property by the government of the host country. To reduce this risk, some companies enter into joint ventures as a way of tapping into foreign markets. The government of the host country or a locally owned firm may go into partnership with a company interested in entering the local market. More and more countries are requiring this type of joint venture as a condition for entering their markets.

Exporting

An alternative to foreign-based operations is exporting. Exporting accomplishes the objective of selling in foreign markets without the large risk of locating operations in foreign countries. The opening of markets in eastern countries, along with the increasing demand for U.S. consumer products worldwide, has made exporting even more enticing. Many companies establish export departments and sell directly to foreign firms. These departments contact foreign buyers, conduct marketing research, and arrange distribution and export documentation. Foreign distribution may be through manufacturers' representatives, import jobbers, dealers, wholesalers, or retailers who function overseas in the same way as their counterparts in the United States. Their duties are described in Chapter 6. As companies become more proficient at exporting, they may begin to explore possibilities for foreign operations. Rather than direct exporting, companies may work through intermediaries. Trading companies are private or government-owned organizations that buy and sell products in much the same way as merchant wholesalers and wholesale dealers/merchandise brokers. These companies may place orders with exporters for their own accounts or for a client. Some of these companies offer a whole range of services to their clients, including importing, exporting, storing, transporting, and distribution through intermediaries.

One of the biggest headaches small and mid-size exporters have had in the past has been financing. Many banks do not understand the complexities of operating in foreign markets, and those who do are unwilling to spend the hours it takes to set up letters of credit. Regional and foreign-based banks have handled export financing in the past. Today factors, forfaiters, and export trading companies help satisfy the need of exporters to finance their sales and get paid faster. Factors recognize foreign receivables and give the exporter 85 percent of the money owed if the transaction is insured by the Export-Import Bank in Washington. Forfaiters accept foreign receivables and give the exporter most of the money before they collect from the buyer when it's backed by a government guarantee. Export trading companies take title to the exports and complete the transaction by shipping the goods and collecting payment. These types of financial companies will facilitate more export trade and will also provide job opportunities themselves.

Foreign Licensing

Still another option, particularly attractive to small companies that cannot afford to invest capital in foreign operations, is foreign licensing. A company will license its concept, which can be a product or a process, to a foreign company that already has facilities and understands the market. In return, the business receives royalties that can range from $\frac{1}{8}$ of 1 percent to 15 percent. In addition to royalties, the company may get valuable feedback in research and development and marketing from the foreign licensee.

CAREERS IN GLOBAL MARKETING

Careers in global marketing do not necessarily mean extensive travel. Most multinational companies prefer to fill positions in foreign countries with citizens of that country and may even be required to do so. The practicality is obvious. Natives speak the language, understand the customs, are paid on a local scale, and do a better job of representing the company than would foreigners. More than likely, graduates in international business, especially at entry-level positions, will be based in the United States while dealing with companies abroad. Though lacking in the glamour desired by many young single people, positions in the United States do not present such complications as homesickness or education for school-aged children. There are many reasons to enter the field of global marketing, including challenges and growing opportunities. However, it is important to understand that though upper-level managers may be posted abroad or travel abroad frequently, entry- and lower-level personnel will probably be based in the United States.

Companies based in one country become multinational when they begin to produce and sell goods in other countries. When their operations extend around the world they are referred to as global enterprises. Much groundwork must be done to select and enter foreign markets successfully. The economic, technological, sociocultural, and political environments in which the business must operate differ greatly from country to country, making the activities of global marketing discussed below considerably more complex.

Global marketing research. Although marketing research professionals perform roughly the same duties described in Chapter 2, their work is much more complicated. They must first obtain information from secondary sources. Useful data may be obtained from such organizations as the United Nations, the U.N. World Health Organization, the U.N. Food and Agriculture Organization, the Organization for Economic Cooperation and Development, and regional trading blocs (e.g., European Community, Association of South East Asian Nations, and Andean Common Market). Governments in foreign countries and U.S. embassies can provide useful information. Researchers also check with nongovernment sources such as banks, international trade clubs, and executives of companies doing business in the country. However, much of this information may have been estimated or crudely collected and must be carefully analyzed to determine whether or not primary data should be collected.

Collecting primary data is even trickier than analyzing the secondary data. While many marketing research techniques may be adapted for use in developed countries, they may be totally unsuitable for use in developing countries with high illiteracy rates, unreliable postal and telephone service, language barriers, and a general suspicion of people asking a lot of questions. To determine which techniques would be appropriate for use in a country, marketing researchers must be familiar with economic, technological, sociocultural, and political factors within the country. Language skills are invaluable since many sources of information will be in the language of the country.

Global product management. The product decisions made for products to be marketed abroad are complex. Members of the project management team have three alternatives regarding product development. The least costly is product standardization, in which the identical product is sold both at home and abroad. This is only effective if the product is suitable for foreign markets. A second strategy is adaptation, in which a product is modified or adapted to suit local tastes and uses. Finally, product innovation, in which a product is especially designed for each foreign market, is sometimes the best route. The team must also grapple with name, distribution, packaging, pricing, and promotion decisions.

Global promotion. Advertising, sales promotion, publicity, and personal selling must take into account attitudes of consumers, competitors, intermediaries, and governments. Clearly, what approach will be effective and even allowed depends on an accurate assessment of these attitudes. Global companies can use ad agencies in their home country, local agencies, or a global advertising agency with branches in numerous countries. United States–based ad agencies have been opening branches in foreign countries for many years. The employees in these branches are hired from the local population. Personal selling is even more culture-bound than advertising. Therefore, sales of consumer products are conducted by local nationals who understand cultural preferences and etiquette in their country. Many manufacturers of expensive industrial products and pharmaceuticals employ U.S. sales representatives who work abroad, but they must study the habits and behaviors of their customers in order to be effective.

GLOBAL E-COMMERCE AND TELESERVICES

Opportunities created by advanced communications and Internet technology are global, but United States–based marketers are only beginning to capitalize on them. Part of the reason for the delay is that the majority of the market is in the United States, where there are more Internet users than in the rest of the world combined. Other factors include government regulations and tariffs, poor infrastructure, high phone rates, and language differences. But Internet usage outside the United States is increasing rapidly. Strong consumer interest is being noted in countries like China and Latin America.[7] Companies like FedEx, Gateway, and Ford are leading the way in global E-commerce and other companies are following. Websites are being adapted for different countries with local language and cultural considerations.

The new Global Alliance Program launched by GE Global exchange Services (GXS) is designed to build relationships among business-to-business E-commerce companies around the world by offering opportunities for joint marketing and joint development of customer relationships. The program focuses on four market segments: software providers, technology providers, consultants, and value-added resellers who all adopt GXS products.[8] The website for the Sydney 2000 Olympic Games was expanded to offer not only information about the games but online advertising and sponsorship opportunities for Olympic sponsors and Internet-based companies.[9] Tapping into the potential of the World Wide Web has only just begun.

Teleservices also provide an opportunity for expansion into Europe, where steady growth in call centers is occurring. Like European call centers, United States–based call centers will have to address the wide range of cultures, languages, and currencies in Europe, as well as the varying public telecommunications infrastructures and Internet usage. Despite these obstacles, U.S. companies are tempted by overtures from European nations such as the United Kingdom, Ireland, the Netherlands, Scandinavia, and Belgium to locate customer contact facilities abroad. U.S. companies may begin by partnering with local consortiums, external service providers, systems integrators, or consultancies to identify opportunities and the best ways to interface with customers. Websites can be used as a tool to support call center sales.[10]

OPPORTUNITIES IN GLOBAL MARKETING

Demand in multinational companies is increasing for MBAs and consultants with expertise in company restructuring and marketing strategy. According to EUREKA 2000–2001 reports, salaries ranged from $2,125 to over $7,250 per month in 1998 for managers in Asia Pacific countries and from $3,650 to $7,916 per month in Europe. Positions abroad are offered to those who have mastered their firm's domestic marketing operations and can speak the language and understand the customs of the country in which they will be based. Travel abroad is usually associated with high-level managers, managers or owners of advertising agencies with operations abroad, owners of export/import businesses, sales representatives of industrial and pharmaceutical products, and fashion coordinators and buyers for stores featuring foreign fashion lines. Foreign-based career opportunities are increasing as more corporations create and expand global operations.

Universities are beginning to orient courses toward global marketing and are sponsoring more study abroad. Today, leading business schools are sending students overseas in their executive MBA programs. Most programs abroad are conducted in partnership with local schools. University of Chicago was the first business school to base an entire executive MBA program abroad. The program was designed to attract managers from all over Europe. University of Chicago staffs the courses with its own Chicago faculty who will research international business problems and take this knowledge back to their students in the United States. Normally, MBA students are sponsored by their companies who help pay tuition and allow time off from work to attend classes. Job applicants interested in positions abroad should inquire in job interviews about such programs. Many employees abroad work for small firms, so opportunities with small companies should not be overlooked.

Foreign internships are available abroad for American students wanting international experience. Students live and work in a foreign country as part of exchange programs that last from six weeks to eighteen months. Students interested in global marketing should become proficient in a language and systematically collect information on countries and industries of interest. The annual *Directory of Overseas Summer Jobs*, published by Peterson's Guides, Inc., is a useful resource found in some libraries and career centers.

Opportunities are increasing for recent graduates who would like to work in Japan, but candidates must be fluent in Japanese and have a technical skill. DISCO International Career Resources, a subsidiary of a Japanese search firm based in Boston, helps Japanese companies recruit students through job fairs. The demand for Americans to work in Asia is predicted to rise in the future because of the lack of universities in nations such as Malaysia, Taiwan, and South Korea to educate sufficient numbers of technical workers.

SOURCES OF INFORMATION

Those who are interested in international marketing can gain more information about the field from international marketing associations such as those listed below:

American Association of Exporters and Importers
51 East Forty-Second Street, 7th floor
New York, NY 10017-5404

International Trade Club of Chicago
c/o The World Trade Center Chicago
Suite 2400 The Merchandise Mart
200 World Trade Center Chicago
Chicago, IL 60654

International Trade Council
3114 Circle Hill Road
Alexandria, VA 22305-1606

International Traders Association
c/o The Mellinger Company
P.O. Box 956
Santa Clarita, CA 91380-9056
Website: www.tradezone.com

World Trade Center of New Orleans
2 Canal Street, Suite 2900
New Orleans, LA 70130

Canada–United States Business Association
600 Renaissance Center, Suite 1100
Detroit, MI 48243

Several directories offer information on companies doing business abroad, including *Directory of European Retailers*, *Directory of American Firms Operating in Foreign Countries*, *Directory of Foreign Firms Operating in the U.S.*, *Principal International Businesses*, and *The World Marketing Directory*. In addition, Surrey Books, Inc. has published *How to Get a Job in Europe* by Robert Sanborn. This book is part of a series that offers information on jobs in the Pacific Rim and in various cities around the United States. Another publication, *The Almanac of International Jobs and Careers* by Ronald L. Krannick and Caryl Rae Krannick, gives information on organizations abroad that hire U.S. citizens.

1. McDonough, Edward F., III, and David Cedrone. "Meeting the Challenge of Global Team Management." *Research Technology Management* 43 (July 2000): 12–17.
2. "Conference Call." *American Demographics, Inc.* 19 (January 1999): 11.
3. "Q & A: Ask the Expert." *Advertising Age International*, March 8, 1999, 8.
4. Nelson, Emily, and Miriam Jordan. "Seeking New Markets for Tampons, P & G Faces Cultural Barriers." *The Wall Street Journal*, December 8, 2000, A1, A8.
5. "CommonHealth Global Services to Be Led by Former EURO RSGG Top Executive." *Business Wire*, August 5, 1999.
6. Willis, Andrew. "Canadian Heads #1 Money Manager's Global Marketing." *Canadian Press Newswire*, November 24, 1999.
7. "Cognitive Releases Q2 2000 Pulse of the Customer Research Findings." *Business Wire*, May 8, 2000.
8. "GE Global Exchange Services Launches Global Alliance Program." *PR Newswire*, August 2, 2000.
9. "SOCOG and IBM Unveil Official Web Site for Sydney 2000 Olympic Games." *Business Wire*, September 14, 1999.
10. Kopf, David. "Hopping the Pond." *TeleProfessional* 12 (February 1999): 33–34, 36.

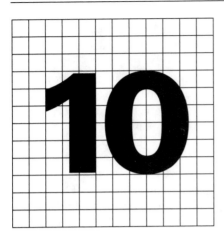

CAREERS IN EDUCATION, CONSULTING, ENTERPRENEURSHIP, AND FRANCHISING

A career is often an amalgam of work experience in varied positions and many different areas. Consider the career of Elliot S. Schreiber, president and CEO of The Alliance for Converging Technologies, a research and consulting firm focusing on strategies in a digital economy. Along with university teaching and international consulting, he held executive positions in three different industries over a twenty-year period in sales, advertising, marketing strategy, brand management, and corporate communications.[1]

Working in a large corporate environment is not for everyone. Some people are mavericks who require greater autonomy in a work atmosphere. A marketing background often leads individuals to pursue careers in higher education, consulting, or entrepreneurship. Many business students feel that operating their own business is the best way to attain their goals, although they doubt that they will actually end up operating their own businesses. The careers described in this chapter are not for beginners but can be viable goals with the proper education and experience. Most successful entrepreneurs have worked for others and gained important knowledge and skills before striking out on their own. This chapter will explore some interesting career alternatives.

MARKETING EDUCATION

Marketing educators are found teaching in many different types of educational settings with varying requirements associated with each. The more common settings include colleges and universities.

Graduate Degree Requirements

Professional educators in the field of marketing find positions in two- and four-year colleges that have marketing courses or programs of study. A master's degree in marketing is usually sufficient qualification to find a teaching position in a community college. Depending on supply and demand, a doctorate might be required and is always preferred. A doctorate in marketing is always required for tenure-track positions in four-year colleges and universities. Earning one's doctorate requires a large commitment both of time and money. After a four-year bachelor's program, a master's program requiring at least two years of full-time study must be undertaken. Successful completion of a masters-level program does not always guarantee admission to a doctoral program.

Applicants must not only have the ability to successfully complete graduate courses in marketing, but they must also achieve a high enough score on the Graduate Management Admissions Test (GMAT) and demonstrate the potential for conducting original research. Doctoral programs require at least two years of full-time coursework and seminars along with the design and completion of a doctoral dissertation. This can be a lengthy process, and a committee must approve each stage before the candidate may go on. A review of the literature, design of the project, data gathering or laboratory experimentation, and an analysis of results can take well over a year to complete.

The reputation of the university and its doctoral program, along with the student's assigned major professor, are factors that come into play when recent recipients of doctorates apply to prestigious and well-known universities. Therefore, those seeking doctorates should carefully evaluate a school and its program before entering. Finding a major professor who shares a student's research interests and who is well known in the field can make doctoral study easier and more valuable. It can also make the student more marketable when entering the job market.

As the demand for marketing professionals increases, so increases the demand for marketing educators. Unfortunately, the number of new business Ph.D.s has grown only 3.5 percent over the past decade, and of the 1,104 in 1999, only half entered academia. In 2001, about 250 positions were vacant in the top thirty business schools, and adding vacancies in the twenty second-tier schools brings the number to more than 400.[2] College enrollments are predicted to grow 22 percent over the next ten years as the echo boomers, children of the baby boomers, enter college.[3] This growth will increase the need for business professors even more.

Demand may vary by area of specialization. Doctoral candidates may concentrate in marketing research, marketing management, purchasing, and so forth. Recent graduates are considered for positions as instructors or assistant professors. Selection criteria can include dissertation and other research, publications, evaluations of professors, and experience outside the doctoral program such as previous employment in marketing areas. In addition, teaching evaluations may be considered since many doctoral students teach undergraduate marketing classes as part of their graduate assistantships.

Responsibilities and Advancement

Instructors in two-year schools primarily teach, but they also may be expected to write books and articles. University professors normally have lighter teach-

Figure 10.1 University College of Business Hierarchy

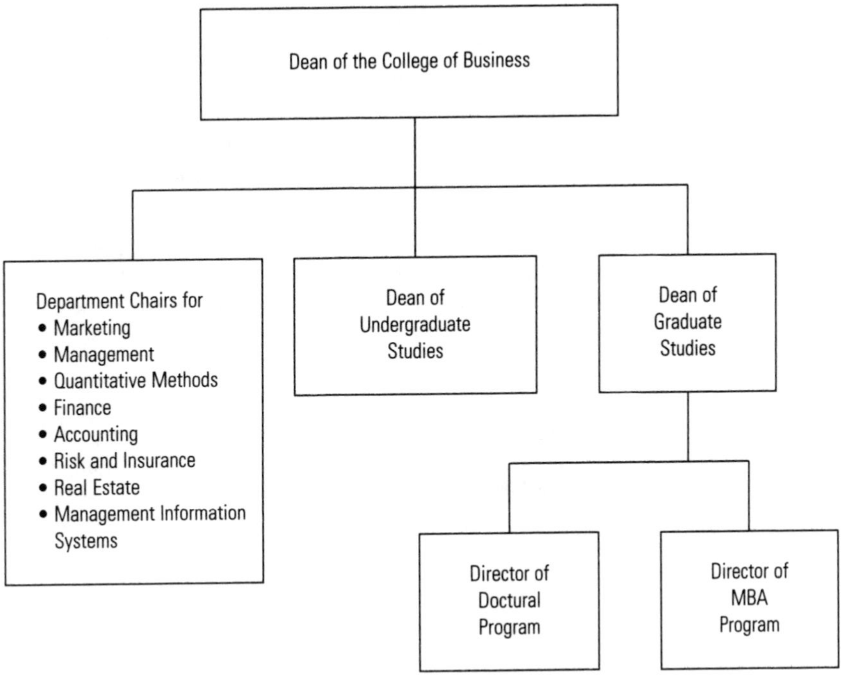

```
                    ┌─────────────────────────────────┐
                    │   Dean of the College of Business │
                    └─────────────────────────────────┘
                                    │
        ┌───────────────────────────┼───────────────────────────┐
┌─────────────────────┐  ┌─────────────────┐  ┌─────────────────┐
│ Department Chairs for│  │     Dean of      │  │     Dean of      │
│ • Marketing          │  │  Undergraduate   │  │    Graduate      │
│ • Management         │  │     Studies      │  │     Studies      │
│ • Quantitative Methods│ └─────────────────┘  └─────────────────┘
│ • Finance            │                              │
│ • Accounting         │                 ┌────────────┴────────────┐
│ • Risk and Insurance │        ┌─────────────────┐  ┌─────────────────┐
│ • Real Estate        │        │   Director of    │  │   Director of    │
│ • Management Information│      │    Doctural      │  │      MBA         │
│   Systems            │        │    Program       │  │    Program       │
└─────────────────────┘        └─────────────────┘  └─────────────────┘
```

ing loads but are required to publish articles in their field as a requirement for promotion and tenure. In addition, both instructors and professors are evaluated on service to their schools, which usually includes serving on committees and can involve fund-raising. Assistant professors are promoted to associate professor, then full professor. Often college professors enter administrative positions such as marketing department chair or dean. Dean of undergraduate or graduate business studies or dean of the college of business administration, as well as other deanships on a college campus, are sometimes filled by former marketing professors. Figure 10.1 shows the organization of a typical university college of business. It is not unusual for professors to earn money outside the university as consultants and sometimes entrepreneurs. Super Lube, a large quick oil change franchise, was started by two Florida State University professors—one in marketing and one in real estate.

MARKETING CONSULTING

Large companies spend millions on consulting and research services. Consulting firms such as Arthur Andersen provide these services. As companies grow, shrink, restructure, and begin global operations, they employ consultants to help with these transitions. Marketing consultants are problem solvers with both extensive experience in marketing and an area of expertise, such as marketing strategy, marketing research, advertising, sales, or merchandising. Businesses and industries hire consultants to help plan marketing strategies and solve problems when strategies go awry. Consulting firms and independent consultants in the United States and Canada are listed in *Consultants and Consulting Organizations Directory*, found in the reference section of libraries. Companies hire marketing consultants mostly in the areas of marketing strategy, market and product research, and feasibility studies.

What consultants do. Since consultants work for many clients, they are exposed to different methods of solving problems and a variety of valuable sources of information. Consultants use diverse experiences to analyze and solve problems for clients. Having knowledge of what works and what doesn't work in a variety of situations, the consultant can make recommendations that can save time and money. Most consultants have tremendous freedom over their time and resources. Whether they freelance, work in small companies, or work for large consulting firms, they work very independently with individual clients. In order to be rehired by a client, a consultant must demonstrate the ability to help solve the client's problems in both creative and cost-effective ways. Consulting is not the job for someone who wants to work less and avoid the nine-to-five routine. Longer, though less routine hours are required for successful consulting. Often client companies impose difficult-to-meet deadlines and expect unrealistic results.

Trends in consulting. Corporate downsizing and growth in the Internet economy has created considerable demand for outside consulting work. Even with declining demand for consultants in the dot-com sector, demand for management analysts will grow faster than average. Consultants with technological skills in Web-enabled customer relationship management and supply-chain management systems will be sought after along with those with skills in the new wireless technology.[4] Change management and corporate reengineering are areas in the consulting business usually in demand. Reengineering in Europe and in corporations around the rest of the globe will offer opportunities abroad for consultants. Emphasis on hiring and retaining skilled employees through compensation and rewards is a greater priority in many companies. In 2000, Watson Wyatt Canada acquired the National Compensation Strategy & Rewards Group of KPGM Consulting to expand its offering in human capital consulting and to focus on E-business integration in Canada and globally.[5]

Once, consultant work was narrow in scope and the consultant worked alone. Today, consultants team up with managers and work together to analyze and solve problems. Companies who have downsized management positions use consultants to complete projects that would have been done by in-house people. Assignments may be short-term or may last years and involve crucial strategy, operations, organization, and technology management. Consultants working on longer projects can be paid high fees. However, executives are expecting more for their money in terms of positive results.

Finding clients. A consultant competes with other consultants for jobs. Though the use of consultants may greatly benefit a business, it is not required for doing business and is one of the first budget items to be cut in hard times. Therefore, consultants must sell their services aggressively. Consultants use a number of promotional techniques to obtain clients: personal relationships and networking, participation in seminars, mailing and phoning, door-to-door selling, advertising, marketing agents, and public relations companies.

Unless a company is rehiring a consultant who has worked for it previously, the company will usually screen and interview a number of consultants. For large contracts, company representatives will visit recent client sites and ask for evidence that the consultant produced results. Who is hired depends on a number of factors. The first is how well the company managers and consultants get along personally since they will usually be working together as a team. The quality of the consultant's references, including companies (probably not competitors) for whom the consultant has completed an assignment similar to the one proposed, is another primary consideration. Although consultants may work for competing companies, consulting contracts often stipulate that they may not disclose privileged company information or work for a competing firm for a certain time period. Finally, the number of years of experience and the quality of that experience are considered.

Sometimes consultants hire consulting broker firms to locate clients. Brokers normally earn 25 to 40 percent of what the consultant earns on the initial contact with the hiring company and less on subsequent contacts. Consulting fees vary greatly depending on the scope and complexity of the project and the reputation of the consultant. Well-established, successful consultants rarely want for employment. Building a reputation as a consultant requires hard work over a number of years.

Working for a consulting firm. Because people are the greatest resource in consulting companies, everyone in large consulting companies gets involved in recruiting new employees. In general, consultants enter the field with two to four years of experience and a college degree, often an MBA or doctorate. Top consulting firms hire graduates from the best business schools and then train them. These firms also offer summer internships to promising candidates and evaluate these recruits before offering them permanent employment with the firm.

Work in large consulting firms is characterized by pressure, long hours, travel, and high turnover. These firms are partnerships that follow an up-or-out policy; that is, consultants have from five to seven years to make partner. If they fail, they are out. Only one in five who begin work with a large company are expected to make partner. Many opt for consulting with large firms for the training and experience first, then go out on their own by choice. Most consulting firms are based in the Northeast and California. Larger firms have branches throughout the country.

Companies often retain consultants on a continuing basis, so consulting work tends to be long-term. Entry-level consulting work in large companies is primarily research. As junior consultants or associates demonstrate the analytic, interpersonal, and motivational skills required for success in the job, they are promoted to the position of case team leader or senior consultant. In this capacity, a consultant supervises a small team normally working on one or two cases at a time. Three or four years later, if the senior consultant is performing well, he or she is promoted to consulting manager. As manager, a consultant leads a consulting team on important client projects. Once promoted to junior partner and finally senior partner or director, the consultant's work is primarily marketing the firm and its services. Figure 10.2 shows a career path in a large consulting firm.

According to EUREKA 2000–2001 figures, entry pay for management consultants in 1998 ranged from $2,516 to $2,975 per month; experienced pay from $3,291 to $3,975; and top pay from $5,000 to over $6,666. Pay for strategic consultants ranged from $6,797 to $10,055 per month, and partners in consulting firms earned from $8,333 per month to over $25,000 per month. An MBA is required for entry into top consulting firms, but beginners may be hired out of college with undergraduate degrees for consulting work. Competition is stiff among large consulting firms in recruiting top graduates. Beginning consultants with MBAs from top business schools such as Harvard and Stanford earn huge salaries plus bonuses. Salaries increase dramatically with promotions, and partners in top consulting firms can earn salaries in excess of $1 million. Independent consultant pay varies considerably depending on the area of expertise and the number of hours worked.

Independent consulting. The number of small consulting operations with no more than three people has increased over the years. Estimates are that only one in five will succeed. Success will depend in part on how well consultants can use the new technology, especially electronic networks, to gain information. Independent consulting may be done on a full-time or part-time basis. Many university professors consult to supplement their university salaries. Retired executives or executives between jobs are in demand as consultants. A marketing-strategy consultant should have been employed as a successful marketing manager in a position fairly high up in an organization before seeking independent status. Although consultants are well paid when they work, paying the bills requires steady work. Self-employed consultants must earn 50 percent more than their large-firm counterparts to pay for the costs of doing business and the benefits normally provided by the company such as health insurance, paid holidays and vacations, travel expenses, office space, supplies and equipment, clerical help, and telephone expenses.

SOURCES OF INFORMATION FOR CONSULTANTS

Numerous publications are available to those interested in consulting as a profession. Consultants are listed in a number of directories, including *Dun's Con-*

Figure 10.2 Career Path in a Large Consulting Firm

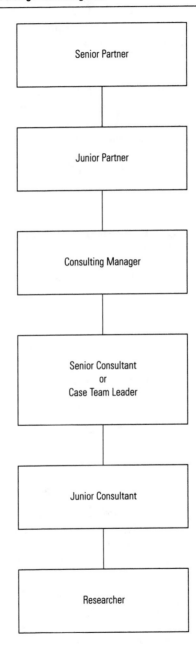

sultant's Directory and *Consultants and Consulting Organizations Directory*, found in the reference section of the library. *Consultants News* and *Journal of Management Consulting* are periodicals covering up-to-date information in the field. Some associations for consultants are listed below:

American Consultants League
30466 Prince William Street
Princess Anne, MD 21853

Association of Management Consulting Firms
380 Lexington Avenue, Number 1699
New York, NY 10168-0002
Website: www.amcf.org

Institute of Management Consultants
1200 19th Street NW, Suite 300
Washington, DC 20036-2428
Website: www.imcusa.org

National Association of Business Consultants
9438 U.S. Highway 19 N, Suite 101
Port Richey, FL 34668
Website: www.nabc-inc.com

Professional and Technical Consultants Association
849-B Independence Avenue
Mountain View, CA 94043
Website: www.patca.org

ONLINE JOB SERVICES FOR INDEPENDENT CONTRACTORS

According to Edie Rasell of the Economic Policy Institute, an amazing 30 percent of the United States' workforce is made up of nonstandard workers, including temporary workers, on-call workers, day laborers, leased workers, the self-employed, and independent contractors.[6] To tap into this reservoir of talent, the Internet offers skills auctions, job sites, resume sites, and recruiters. The auctions offer independent contractors bids for their services, though not always at the pay rates they would like. Internet companies such as eLance.com, Monster.com, Bid4Geeks.com, and HotDispatch.com are part of what is becoming a saturated field. The fastest growing worldwide service for independent contractors with over 45,000 freelancers and 15,000 project managers, Ants.com, has become partners with MarketingJobs.com, which specializes in marketing, sales, and advertising jobs.[7]

ENTREPRENEURSHIP

Confidence in themselves and their ideas is what propels entrepreneurs into business against all odds. Kate Spade and her husband Andy used his $35,000 in savings to produce the high fashion handbags that women purchase for hundreds of dollars in upscale department stores. Kate Spade Inc. today operates its own retail stores in New York, Los Angeles, Boston, and Tokyo.[8] Sue Rodin was inspired by the 1996 Olympic Games in Atlanta. She watched as the American women's teams won gold medals for both basketball and soccer, and then signed Julie Foudy, cocaptain of the women's soccer team, as the first client for her new agency.[9] Many people start new businesses every year. Some new business start-ups are by those who lost their jobs as a result of downsizing, but most were by individuals seeking a better quality of life than they are able to find working for someone else. New entrepreneurs are characterized by being better educated and having more sophisticated businesses than in previous years.

New start-ups in E-commerce were plentiful in the late 1990s, but many failed with the downward correction of the economy. The perception that building an Internet business is easy and cheap is not true. In today's economy, capital isn't as easy to obtain, technology is complicated, skilled employees are scarce, and most of the good names have been taken. A success was digIT Interactive Inc., which became one of Canada's top fifty Web-services companies before selling to Nurun, Canada's largest Web-services company and a global player. Correctly anticipating the problems small Web-services companies would face in an uncertain economic future with competition becoming larger and more global, digIT's four major shareholders made a smart decision by selling.[10] Many successful online companies provide consulting or business services to other businesses. Less expensive computer and telecommunications equipment has been a factor contributing to this.

Small businesses are vital to the U.S. economy. According to Bureau of Labor statistics, small businesses account for about half of the nonfarm, nongovernmental employment and about half of the private sector output in the United States. During the 1990s, small businesses generated three-quarters of the growth in jobs. In 1998 the number of small businesses reached an all-time high. Although the number of new start-ups has fallen in four of the last five years, high-tech and Internet-related start-ups are on the rise and are generating enough new jobs to keep employment from start-ups rising. An explanation is that many high-tech start-ups grow more rapidly, having access to broader customer markets, and many are employing 100 people within the first year or so.[11] About 5 percent of the small businesses create most of the jobs. However, apart from job creation, entrepreneurial companies spur large ones to make innovations in products and to create new markets. Consider the impact on technology made by Bill Gates and the impact on retailing made by Sam Walton, the creator of Wal-Mart. Realistically, most of today's small businesses provide only a modest living for their owners. The majority will go out of business within the first three years. Although business terminations in 1998 were up, with 9.4 percent closing, business bankruptcies were down 17.9 percent to the lowest level since 1980.

Entrepreneurs are those individuals who are willing to assume the risks of starting their own businesses. Given this risk, which is considerable, why do they do it? Some frequently given reasons are to use skills or ability, to gain control over one's life, to build for the family, for the challenge, to live in a particular location, to gain respect or recognition, to earn lots of money, and to fulfill others' expectations. Women have been starting businesses at twice the rate of men. More and more African Americans are starting their own companies. A black business network of powerful contacts is helping to drive economic growth in such areas as communications, entertainment, and consumer goods.

Entrepreneurs Start with a Good Idea

The demand for a product or service creates an opportunity for prospective entrepreneurs. Understanding that consumers in the 1990s wanted to be educated, entertained, preserve the environment, be good parents, stay healthy, and feel rich, clever entrepreneurs designed products to meet these needs. Big business leaves many needs unmet and market niches untapped. Entrepreneurs go against the odds every time they start a new business, but that doesn't stop many from succeeding despite those odds. Independent entrepreneurs find a market niche, develop a product, and market it as do large companies. A tremendous amount of knowledge and tireless effort are required to develop a successful small business. Debbi Fields opened her first store in 1977 at the age of twenty with a $50,000 loan from a banker who liked her chocolate chip cookies. Ten years later, Mrs. Fields Inc. was a company of 543 stores in six countries, including Japan and Australia.

Succeeding as an Entrepreneur

Because of the large investment of time and money and the high risk of failure, an entrepreneur must have a total commitment to the business, a tolerance for hard work, good health, and financial backing. The prospective entrepreneur usually seeks financial backing from relatives, friends, and lending institutions. Normally entrepreneurs put a good bit of their own money into their businesses. If they have developed an impressive business plan, they may be successful in getting financial backing from outside sources such as banks or venture capitalists. Venture capital firms are usually groups of investors who extend financial backing annually to start-up companies for part ownership of the company, depending on the terms of each arrangement. Usually the venture capital firm wants to protect its investment by having considerable say in how the company is run. Many small business owners have taken on the risk of starting their own businesses in order to have total freedom to run them as they see fit. When this is the case, the entrepreneur attempts to go it alone, avoiding capital with strings attached.

While securing financial backing is often a huge stumbling block for entrepreneurs, even if it is secured, more than money is required to make a business thrive. Once finances are secured, an entrepreneur begins to implement the business plan. Since in most small businesses the owner is responsible for planning, accounting, purchasing, producing, marketing, staffing, and overall management, a general knowledge of all the activities of business is required. Above all, an entrepreneur must be a salesperson extraordinaire—first selling the idea in order to raise the capital to start the company, then selling the company and its future to prospective employees, and finally selling the product to consumers who are constantly bombarded with ideas for new and better products. Entrepreneurs should be very aware of market and economic conditions if they hope to succeed, and these conditions are constantly changing.

Preparing for Entrepreneurship

Can a person be taught to be an entrepreneur? Probably not. But what can be taught are the skills needed for an entrepreneur to be successful. Because of demand, business schools are adding more courses and encouraging more student participation in entrepreneurial competitions. Some schools offer comprehensive entrepreneurship programs, usually in the form of a concentration of electives. Coursework focuses on the financing of a new business and the commercialization of new products. The best preparation, however, is outside the classroom, working for a company in the same industry that the prospective entrepreneur would like to enter.

SOURCES OF INFORMATION FOR SMALL BUSINESSES

Usually small family businesses employ family members in key positions and, if the business has a board of directors, they are often family members. In such a situation, the question of where to get objective advice on business matters arises. The Small Business Administration (SBA), with offices in all major cities, is an excellent source of information for those who want to start their own businesses or need help once they have set up shop. Numerous brochures published by SBA are available in SBA offices around the country or may be requested by mail. These brochures give valuable how-to information such as developing a business plan, acquiring financing, marketing products, and much more. Many books have been written on managing small businesses. Small business consultants offer services to small business owners who can afford them.

Information and assistance for small business owners can be obtained by writing some of the following:

Chamber of Commerce of the United States
1615 H Street NW
Washington, DC 20062
Website: www.uschamber.com

National Association of Small Business Investment Companies
666 11th Street NW, Number 750
Washington, DC 20001
Website: www.nasbic.org

National Association of Women Business Owners
1411 K Street NW
Washington, DC 20005
Website: www.nawbo.org

National Business Owners Association
820 Gibbon Street, Suite 204
Alexandria, VA 22314
Website: www.nboa.com

National Federation of Independent Business
53 Century Boulevard, Suite 300
Nashville, TN 37214

National Small Business United
1156 15th Street NW, Suite 1100
Washington, DC 20005
Website: www.nsbu.org

Small Business Assistance Center
554 Main Street
P.O. Box 15014
Worcester, MA 01615-0014

Office of Advocacy of U.S. Small Business Administration
409 Third Street SW
Washington, DC 20416
Website: www.sba.gov/advo

FRANCHISING

All types of people opt for franchise ownership. Women tend to start twice as many small businesses as men, yet only a small percentage of franchises—8.5 percent in 1995. It is interesting how people select franchises. Bill Anderson was on the road almost 300 days a year and used Mail Boxes Etc. for shipping during off-hours. He was so impressed with the service that he opened his own, then a second, and at this time plans a third. When Anthony Cracolici was terminated from a job he'd held for twenty years, he and his wife attended a small-business expo where they discovered Happy & Healthy Products, Inc., a company that sells all-natural frozen dessert bars. They bought a franchise and are now master distributors, the highest level of franchise ownership for the company. Tammy Cassman worked for years in retail sales before opening a Fastframe picture-framing franchise, with corporate headquarters offering her training and even helping her clean and organize her store. Ron McBride used his experience in tax law at the Internal Revenue Service to help him succeed with his Triple Check Income Tax Service franchise to which he added a Triple Check Financial Services franchise.[12] All of these successful franchisees built on both positive and negative career experiences to evaluate franchise possibilities and select franchises that best met their professional and personal needs.

Many people want to own a small business but have neither an original idea nor the business acumen to start a business from scratch, so they buy a franchise. A franchise is an agreement between a small business owner and a parent company that gives the owner the right to sell the company's product (goods or services) under conditions agreed upon by both. The store itself is also called a franchise. A great many small retail stores are franchises, including fast food stores, gas stations, and print shops. Statistics show that the proportionate number of failures among franchises is significantly less than small business failures in general. The reason for this difference is that franchises enjoy special advantages over other small business operations.

Advantages to Franchise Ownership

Failure among franchises is reduced by the nature of the franchise itself. Franchises sell nationally known and extensively tested products for which a market has already been established. Training and assistance come from the parent company to help the new owner choose a location, set up shop, estimate potential sales, and design market strategies that have worked in similar locations. Cooperative buying power enables the franchise owner to purchase supplies at lower costs from distributors supplying all franchises of the parent company. Sometimes the parent company helps to establish credit; this is helpful because it usually takes a new business at least six months to turn a profit. Often this period is longer; sometimes a business is never profitable. Even franchises of a successful parent company sometimes fail.

Disadvantages to Franchise Ownership

Franchise owners pay a franchising fee plus a percentage of their profits to the parent company. This percentage is determined by the amount of advertising and consulting support given by the parent company and varies considerably. It can range from 3 percent to a whopping 50 percent in the temporary-help business. However, in the temporary-help business, the franchiser finances the payrolls of the franchisees. The requirement that the owner buy both equipment and supplies from vendors specified by the parent company may prevent the franchise owner from making more economical purchases elsewhere.

Before entering into an agreement, a business owner should read the fine print and get legal advice as well. The law requires that franchisers provide a detailed franchise prospectus to potential franchisees. It is wise to keep in mind that the business of the franchise parent company is selling franchises, and like all businesses, it is going to make the product as appealing as possible. Potential profits and estimated costs of setting up the franchise that are given by the parent company should be confirmed by questioning other franchise owners as well as by other objective sources. The Federal Trade Commission requires that franchisers divulge any litigation in which they are involved. Because fraudulent claims and franchise scams are on the rise, a franchise agreement should be entered into carefully, with legal advice and as much outside knowledge of the parent company as possible.

Growth in Franchises

Continuing growth in small businesses includes franchises. Although mainstream franchises such as hotels, fast-food restaurants, and car-rental agencies have reached a saturation point, new opportunities in business and professional services are available. Manufacturers are franchising aspects of the distribution process such as sales territories and delivery routes in order to reduce overhead. More franchise opportunities will be available partially because it costs less for a company to franchise than it did in the past. Uniform disclosure documents are accepted in all states, reducing legal fees.

Home-based franchises may cost only thousands, while the most expensive franchises can cost millions. The percentage of these costs required in cash varies with current credit conditions and ranges from 20 percent to 40 percent when money is tight. The remaining percentage can be bank-financed and pledged with personal guarantees and collateral. Franchise agreements are not to be entered into lightly. The monetary cost of failure can be considerable.

Some franchises go out of business. Some franchises are bought back by the franchiser or bought by another prospective franchise owner. Franchises fail for many reasons. Lack of financing to support the business until it becomes profitable may cause failure. Even with services and training provided by the franchiser, some owners simply lack the skills required to run a successful business. Often investors buy franchises and hire others to run them. Incentives are different for paid employees than for owners. Thus lack of involvement by the investor is often cited as the major reason for business failure. Sometimes the parent company fails, causing all franchisees to shut down—successful or not.

SOURCES OF INFORMATION ON FRANCHISES

The growth of franchising can be tracked in *Entrepreneur* magazine. The *Franchise Opportunities Handbook* published by the Bureau of Industrial Economics and Minority Business Development Agency of the U.S. Department of Commerce can be found in the government documents section of most libraries. Published monthly, it includes a list of franchises for sale, as well as excellent tips for prospective franchise owners, such as a checklist for evaluating a franchise, financial assistance information, and a bibliography of sources of franchising information. Other sources include the following:

Directory of Franchise Business Opportunities
Franchise Business Opportunities Publishing Company
1725 Washington Road, Suite 205
Pittsburgh, PA 15241

Directory of Franchising Organizations
Pilot Industries, Inc.
347 Fifth Avenue
New York, NY 10016

The Franchise Annual
Info Press
736 Center Street
Lewiston, NY 14092

American Association of Franchisees and Dealers
3636 4th Avenue, Suite 310
San Diego, CA 92103-4237
Website: www.aafd.org

American Franchisee Association
53 West Jackson Boulevard, Suite 205
Chicago, IL 60604
Website: www.franchise.org

International Franchise Association
1350 New York Avenue NW, Suite 900
Washington, DC 20005
Website: www.franchise.org

The directories listed above are revised annually and provide information on many franchise opportunities. These franchises should be investigated thoroughly by contacting both the Better Business Bureau and the International Franchise Association. Many excellent books on franchising are on the market, a number of them available through the International Franchise Association itself.

Online sources of franchise information include Franchise.com for home-based businesses at www.franchise.com, Franchise Database, offering franchise opportunities by type, at www.franchisedatabase.com, and for Canada's home-based entrepreneurs, Home.Biz.CA.

1. "Alliance for Converging Technologies." *Canada News Wire*, February 23, 1999.
2. Merritt, Jennifer. "Brain Drain at the B-Schools." *Business Week*, March 5, 2001, 106.
3. Franecki, David. "Matters of Degree." *The Wall Street Journal*, November 29, 1999, R17.
4. Goff, Leslie. "Surefire Uncertainties." *Computerworld*, January 1, 2001, 39.
5. "Watson Wyatt Acquires KPMG's Canadian Compensation and Rewards Practice." *Canada News Wire*, August 17, 2000.
6. Lewis, Diane E. "Hired! By the Highest Bidder: More Independent Contractors Are Bypassing Employment Agencies, Turning Instead to the Net to Auction Off Their Skills for the Right Pay or Perks." *The Boston Globe*, July 9, 2000, G1.
7. "Ants.com and MarketingJobs.com Partner." *Business Wire*, July 6, 2000.
8. Conlin, Michelle. "It's in the Bag." *Forbes*, December 28, 1999, 86.
9. Cropper, Carol Marie. "Agent for the Women of the Hour." *The New York Times*, July 25, 1999, section 3, 2.
10. Rudyk, Nathan. "Selling Out or Selling Up? A Newly Minted Dot-Com Millionaire Explains His Toughest Decision." *Profit: The Magazine for Canadian Entrepreneurs* 19, no 3 (May 2000): 65.
11. Loftus, Peter. "Start-Up Fever." *The Wall Street Journal*, July 17, 2000, R6.
12. Garrett, Echo Montgomery. "Lifestyles of the Rich & Franchised." *Goldhirsh Group, Inc.*, July 1999, 103.

ECONOMIC TRENDS AND THEIR IMPACT ON MARKETING CAREERS

Now may be the best time for new college graduates to enter the job market. Members of the aging college-educated workforce are beginning to retire, creating an even larger demand at management levels in companies. Understanding trends in marketing and in the economy are particularly important for entry-level job seekers. Major transformations have occurred in American business over the past two decades that impact marketing careers, including the shift to a service economy, the globalization of business, the restructuring of corporations, the impact of communications and network technology, the diversification in the workforce, and changing lifestyles of American families. These transformations affect the types of products offered, the nature of jobs involved in marketing them, the demand for individuals with certain skills, the salaries offered workers, even the sizes and locations of businesses themselves.

Throughout this book, trends related to specific fields were highlighted, salaries and demand statistics cited, and opportunities for individuals in certain areas discussed. This chapter will deal with a larger perspective to facilitate a comparison of job opportunities across the field of marketing.

SERVICES MARKETING

We live in a service-oriented economy. According to Bureau of Labor statistics, marketing and sales jobs will increase 15 percent, or 2.3 million jobs, from 1998 to 2008, and most of these jobs will be in services. Roughly 75 percent of all jobs are in a services industry. Small businesses employ more workers than large ones. Of the 55.4 million employed in small businesses in 1998, 20.4 million worked in services. New college graduates will find opportunities in fields that they may have never considered or know very little about. To better understand marketing opportunities in the services industries, it is necessary to differentiate between a good and a service from a marketing perspective. A service is an activity performed for an individual or a firm. While a physical product is impersonal, a service is highly personal. Its quality is contingent on the performance of the worker and can vary considerably within a firm.

Service marketers direct and implement a service firm's marketing effort. Using marketing researchers to determine the needs of its chosen market and the price customers will pay for the firm's service, service marketers function much like any marketing manager. Service industries may be equipment-based, people-based, or a combination of both. For example, electronic databases, automated bank tellers, and diagnostic medical equipment are the tools of equipment-based service industries. An advertising agency is people-based. Only by motivating and inspiring people can managers assure that the service rendered is top quality.

Marketing services is considerably more challenging than marketing goods. Services are intangible. Banks and airlines cannot give samples or claim qualities that outlast those of the competition. Services go out of existence as they are created. They cannot be repossessed if bills are unpaid. Although services cannot be stored as inventory, they must be produced on demand. Long lines or an inability to accommodate customers can seriously impair a service business. Services cannot be mailed; they must be delivered on the spot at a convenient location. Quality is very hard to control—similar services can vary greatly from organization to organization, employee to employee, and even for the same employee. Everyone has bad days. These unique aspects of services require attention and focus by the marketers in a service industry.

In human-intensive services such as advertising and consulting, the employees are the assets. Service sales representatives perform the same activities as those selling goods, as discussed in Chapters 6 and 7. An important distinction is that service companies gain much of their business through referrals from satisfied customers. A retail store selling goods might lose some business if a salesperson is rude or incompetent. If it is a specialty shop, a customer might return but avoid that particular salesperson. In a service business, the service itself is the product. A customer receiving poor service will not return and will share the dissatisfaction with others. The success of the service firm depends on hiring the best employees. The pressure to deliver high quality service is intense.

Most new college graduates will be employed in service industries. Experts predict continuing high demand for services sales representatives. It is important to identify an industry as well as a field and prepare oneself for its unique demands. Areas where demand will be particularly strong for sales representatives are temporary help services, business and financial services, information services, and advertising sales. Hotel and automotive service sales will also grow at a faster-than-average rate. Competition among professional service firms is affecting hiring practices. More of these companies are hiring marketing directors, coordinators, and business development personnel. The professional service marketing job responsibilities include research, coordinating seminars, and writing brochures.

THE RESTRUCTURING OF AMERICAN CORPORATIONS

The 1980s were a turbulent period in American business causing major restructuring in corporations, much of which continued through the 1990s. Acquisitions and buyouts changed many corporate identities. Recession and competition from abroad forced downsizing and restructuring. Assigning limited resources in a vastly more complex global marketplace is the challenge confronting managers today. The business environment of the next decade will be characterized by an uncertain economy, more global competition, shortened product life cycles, more new competing products, and more demanding customers in terms of quality and convenience. Customer relationship management (CRM) has become a new buzzword. Many companies use CRM systems to collect customer data and provide better service. Entry-level jobs will be more varied and challenging. Managers with too much to do will be forced to delegate many tasks to lower-level and beginning employees. Project teams will be more widely used as companies attempt a more entrepreneurial approach to product development. Work will be less structured. More freedom, as a result of reduced numbers of supervisors, will enable employees to show what they are able to do.

Marketing is a line function. That is, marketing activities result in sales and profit; therefore, marketing will get the lion's share of the available resources. The downsizing of staffs within different departments will contribute to the trend of outsourcing, or contracting out certain types of work. Often outsourcing is more cost effective than maintaining certain departments and staff. Contracting out advertising, sales promotion, and public relations campaigns will become more common, which is good news for the firms offering these services. Marketing and economic research and consulting firms will be positively affected by this trend.

THE IMPACT OF CHANGING TECHNOLOGY AND THE INTERNET

Advances in information and communications technology have revolutionized the workplace of today and created opportunities for companies and individuals that simply did not exist a mere decade ago. Computers are faster, cheaper, smaller, and infinitely more powerful than ever before. New communications technology has enabled managers to make better decisions faster. Sophisticated marketing research analysis such as multivariate statistical analyses, which is too complex to do manually, can be done handily on computers. Monitoring the economic and business environments is easier through the Internet. Advances in manufacturing equipment allow managers to respond more rapidly to competition, and improved distribution and inventory techniques make sales campaigns more efficient and effective. Improved graphics technology has greatly affected the field of advertising. Breakthroughs in telecommunications technology have furthered the development of branch or satellite offices and the expansion of global operations. In short, technological change has dramatically affected every aspect of marketing.

E-commerce continues to grow dynamically with consumer E-commerce growing from $2.0 billion in 1997 to $20.2 billion in 1999 and business-to-business E-commerce growing from $18.6 billion to $176.8 billion over that same time period, according to a study by Forrester Research. Forrester predicts that by 2004, consumer E-commerce will total $185 billion and business-to-business will total $2.7 trillion. Another study by the Center for Research in Electronic Commerce at the University of Texas in Austin shows that the number of people employed in the Internet economy doubled from 1.25 million in 1998 to 2.5 million in 1999. Many technology companies report that over half of their new hires come from referrals from employees who are being rewarded with money, gifts, and trips for their efforts. Forrester also reports that, because online recruiting is more efficient than newspapers or headhunters, companies are increasing their online recruiting 52 percent by 2004 and predictions are that the online recruitment industry will grow from $602 million in 1999 to $7.1 billion by 2005.[1]

CHANGES IN LIFESTYLES AND VALUES

Individual lifestyles and values have been changing over the years. More and more people are viewing work as a way to maintain lifestyle rather than developing lifestyles consistent with work. The family is taking central importance in the choices people make, both in their careers and as consumers. People are marrying and having children later in life when careers are already in place. With an ever-increasing number of two-career couples, both partners share in family responsibilities. Though studies show that it is still the woman who misses work most frequently when children are ill, men are definitely doing more of the shopping. In addition, the divorce rate is decreasing. Participation of women in the workforce has leveled off. The birth rate has risen, new mothers are slower to return to work, and women are staying in school longer.

Placing greater emphasis on the quality of life and personal and professional freedom, many start their own businesses. Women with children often work or run their own businesses at home. Information and communications technology enables companies to allow their employees to work at home. Part-time employment is an option for many. Contingent workers are self-employed or work part-time and include those who do not work 40 hours a week, year-round, or for the same employer. They include a wide variety of workers such as part-time clerks, movie stars, or self-employed doctors and make up a sizable percentage of the workforce. This flexible source of labor makes U.S. business more efficient than its European competitors.

THE JOB MARKET

The job market of today is a bonanza for both the experienced and newcomers. In today's market, changing jobs is common as applicants seek greater compensation and benefits, more challenging work, and growth potential. According to U.S. Department of Labor statistics, the average 32-year-old held nine full- or part-time jobs since entering the job market and workers are changing jobs roughly every two and a half years. Consistent with this finding, a recent survey conducted by Myjobsearch.com revealed that more than two-thirds of workers would leave their current jobs for a 10 percent raise.[2] With a low unemployment rate and plenty of jobs, workers today are managing their careers as businesses, with earnings and profits being key considerations. Individuals, especially those with technology skills, find that changing jobs and even industries is easier since companies use similar tools and strategies for competing in today's global economy. According to a recent WebFeet.com survey, experienced applicants interviewed on average with three companies and received offers from two of them.[3]

The labor force was roughly 140 million at the start of the millennium with an estimated growth of 11 percent between 1996 and 2006 relative to an estimated growth in demand of 19 percent for that same period. A decline in the number of workers ages 24 to 45 is going to create an estimated 30 percent shortage even if a majority of baby boomers work past the age of 65.[4] Employers are using phased retirement programs including shorter workweeks, temporary work, or opportunities to work from home to keep employees longer. Those most in demand will be managers and those with mastery over the technology supporting the global economy. According to Development Dimensions International, the number of managerial jobs will rise 21 percent between 1998 and 2010.[5]

Overall, the demand for business and management majors has been consistently strong. In the areas of sales and marketing, demand has increased, particularly for business-to-business marketers. Marketing professionals are employed throughout the country and abroad by manufacturers, retailers, advertising agencies, consulting and public relations firms, product testing laboratories, business services firms, government, and nonprofit organizations, among others. Those who have mastered the information technology that connects the customer to all the people in the organization will be greatly in demand.

The aging of America is also having an impact on the job market. Though many baby boomers are financially well off enough to retire early, they are also healthy enough to work longer. It is unclear what the overall picture will be in the future regarding older people in the workforce. Today airline pilots are fighting to continue work after 60, the age mandated by the federal government for retirement of pilots. Mentoring of younger employees will become more common, since older managers possess the business acumen needed to run a company. In addition, surveys revealed those over 55 spend more time online than any other age group.[6]

In the past, temporary help was usually clerical in nature. Today, employment agencies can provide a production line for a month or a computer team for a lengthy project. This gives employers flexibility and provides individuals who want to work independently more opportunities. The trend of outsourcing by companies will continue, offering independent contractors and consultants many new opportunities.

Candidates and companies find each other in many ways. Job seekers today still use job advertisements in periodicals, but more and more use online job listings. Headhunters are more plentiful. The increased number of recruiters on college campuses signals increased demand and will greatly help new graduates in their job search. According to a study by Development Dimensions International, over half of all employers planned to spend more on recruitment in 2000 than in 1999.[7] In their "Job Outlook 2001" report, the National Association of Colleges and Employers (NACE) stated that employers plan to increase college hiring by 23.4 percent in 2001.[8] Many individuals contact companies whose ads for products and services attract them rather than ads for posted job openings. In today's market, companies are always looking for qualified candidates and will create jobs for such individuals. Uncertain economic conditions might cause employers to be a little more cautious about adding new positions since hiring and firing costs are growing.

TRENDS IN EMPLOYMENT AND COMPENSATION

Opportunities in marketing careers exist virtually all over the world in companies of all sizes. However, considerable trade-offs in terms of quality of life, cost of living, and the merits of the job must all be considered. As expected, salaries in marketing tend to be highest where the cost of living is greatest. For example, in Seattle, the city that tops the list in fastest-rising home prices, marketing professionals earn the following average annual salaries with the indicated years of experience:

Marketing Assistant with 2 to 4 years, $36,434–$49,829

Marketing Research Analyst with 0 to 4 years, $40,708–$74,204

Communications Manager with 7 years, $55,430–$86,317

Marketing Manager with 7 years, $63,533–$97,364

Product/Brand Manager with 7 years, $68,634–$94,237

Source: *The San Francisco Chronicle*, June 23, 2000, p. B3.

Money magazine placed San Francisco and New York at the top of their "best places to live" list in 1999. For 2000, *Money* focused on cities with vibrant economies and job growth, but who are successfully managing growth and providing a high quality of life including good schools, low crime, green space, cultural outlets, and an accessible city center. Portland, Oregon, tops its list for big cities and Sarasota, Florida, was named the best small city. Regional top honors go to Providence, Rhode Island, for the Northeast; Chicago, Illinois, for the Midwest; Raleigh/Durham/Chapel Hill, North Carolina, for the South; and Salt Lake City, Utah, for the West.

In general, larger companies with more than 500 employees pay higher salaries than smaller ones. The Bureau of Labor statistics reports that the gap in pay widened over the past decade to almost a 50 percent higher pay rate in large companies by 1998, with a wage increase of 3.3 percent from March 1998 to March 1999 compared to one of 2.3 percent for small companies over that same period.[9] Although closing the pay gap somewhat, women still earn significantly less than men for the same work in almost every job in every industry, according to *Working Woman* magazine's twentieth salary survey. Big gains were made by female media directors who now earn $.90 for every $1 made by men for the same job, up 6 percent from 1999.[10] In Canada, above average sales and marketing salaries in every industry are highly correlated with higher corporate profits.[11] A number of websites provide salary information including The Salary Center, a collaboration of monster.com and Robert Half International Inc. at salarycenter.monster.com and salary.com.

Business students today are confidant that they will find good jobs in the current economy. Top industry choices include management consulting, investment banking, and E-business consulting, according to WebFeet.com's Campus Pulse study conducted in October 2000. The study further revealed that college and business students are demanding much higher salaries. For example, MBAs expect, on average, a compensation package of $122,500 including a signing bonus of $20,200, and undergraduates expect compensation of $57,200 with a $5,700 signing bonus.[12] The reality for business graduates in Canada in 1999, according to the Business $ense/HayGroup Annual Business Grad Salary Survey, is that salaries ranged from $23,000 for new undergraduates to $100,000 for MBAs; only 13 percent of Canadian companies offer signing bonuses to MBAs with experience and 7 percent to undergraduates. Key factors that Canadian employers consider in hiring are relevant areas of study, fit with the organizational culture, and growth potential.[13]

For new graduates in marketing, salaries can increase by over $3,000 a year for the same job, depending on geographical area. Salaries for similar work vary from industry to industry according to industry norms. Since employers within an industry are competing for the same workers, salaries are somewhat consistent but vary according to the size of the company and the budgets of the different departments. For example, the larger the budget for a certain product, the larger the salaries of those working on the development and promotion of it. Within service industries, firms providing engineering and research services usually pay more than other service firms. The National Association of Colleges and Employers (NACE) surveys job offers to new college graduates. This information can be found in many college career centers or can be obtained by writing NACE at 61 Highland Avenue, Bethlehem, PA 18017-9085 or accessing its website at www.naceweb.org.

Figure 11.1 presents average yearly salaries offered to graduates in marketing-related areas.

Figure 11.1 Average Salaries for New Graduates in 1999

Function	Salary	% Change from 1998
Advertising	$28,962	6.1
Brand/Product Management	37,304	19.0
Buyer/Merchandising	35,500	10.5
Customer Service	31,135	16.3
Design/Graphic Arts	33,619	15.7
Distribution	35,978	5.7
Market Research	34,030	3.0
Media Planning	30,271	8.5
Public Relations	31,240	18.2
Purchasing	40,311	24.8
Sales	33,143	4.8
MBA nontechnical	50,276	0.4
MBA technical	54,225	−1.1
Masters in marketing/marketing management (including market research)	45,593	NA

Source: NACE Salary Survey, Fall 2000, vol. 39, issue 4.

In researching salary figures it is not unusual for different surveys measuring the same thing to yield different figures because the sample groups differ. The figures reported throughout this book were used because they are consistent with the overall picture presented in a number of sources, but they, too, should be considered approximations.

Salary is only part of the compensation picture. In response to employee demands, employers are offering better and more varied benefit packages. Some of the following items, plus numerous others, may be included in the package: health insurance, dental insurance, life insurance, disability insurance, vacation, sick leave, paid holidays, bonuses, pension plans, employee stock ownership and/or stock purchase plans, and profit-sharing plans. Even in a declining economy, *Fortune* magazine's best 100 companies to work for in 2001 are continuing to offer enticing perks. Of these companies, twenty-six provide on-site day care, twenty-nine offer concierge services such as dry-cleaning pickup, forty-seven give domestic-partner benefits to same-sex couples, and thirty-one give fully paid sabbaticals. In addition, eighty-three offer money for referring new hires, as much as $15,000 at three of these companies.[14] Job applicants must evaluate benefit packages to compute total compensation.

Many important job factors should be considered before an individual accepts a position with a firm. Compensation alone is not enough to base an employment decision. In addition to evaluating compensation, company training and development opportunities are also important benefits that should be carefully evaluated as part of a job offer. It is very important for those entering the job market to investigate companies thoroughly and to ask probing questions during the job interview. Chapter 12 will provide sources of information and job-seeking hints.

1. Rubin, Jeff. "Forget Stock Options, Referrals Are the Recruiter's Latest Weapon." *The Wall Street Journal*, August 1, 2000, B16.
2. "Myjobsearch.com Reveals New Trend in Employee Loyalty." *Business Wire*, January 20, 2000.
3. "Pounding the Pavement in Search of a Job? Probably Not, According to New WebFeet.com Study." *PR Newswire*, October 10, 2000.
4. Hube, Karen. "Help Wanted." *The Wall Street Journal*, November 29, 1999, R20, R25.
5. Dierdorff, Jack. "Brain Drain." *Business Week*, September 20, 1999, 114.
6. Dierdorff, Jack. "Brain Drain." *Business Week*, September 20, 1999, 124.
7. "Myjobsearch.com Reveals New Trend in Employee Loyalty." *Business Wire*, January 20, 2000.
8. Bennett, Julie. "In Pursuit of Personnel: Search Firms Reinvent Recruitment." *The Wall Street Journal*, January 23, 2001, B16.
9. Mandel, Michael. "Big Players Offer Better Pay." *Business Week*, August 30, 1999, 30.
10. Joyner, Tammy. "Survey Says Women Make Strides, But Still Face Salary Gap." *The Atlanta Journal and Constitution*, July 4, 2000.
11. "Bosses Pay More to Get More." *Canadian Press Newswire*, May 19, 2000.
12. "In Spite of Dot Com Shakeout, Career Confident Graduates Expect Lofty Salaries and Signing Bonuses, New WebFeet.com Survey Finds." *PR Newswire*, January 9, 2001.
13. "What Do Employers Look for in Business Graduates?" *Canada NewsWire*, January 10, 2000.
14. Levering, Robert, and Milton Moskowitz. "The Best 100 Companies to Work For." *Fortune*, January 8, 2001, 148–158.

BEGINNING A SUCCESSFUL CAREER IN MARKETING

Smart new business graduates today understand that the likelihood of success in a marketing career depends on two things: getting the skills employers seek and finding a good first job. The Internet has given students incredible access to the information needed to do this. Employers today place skills above everything else when hiring. Preparing for a career in marketing involves acquiring these skills through educational programs and gaining experience through part-time jobs, internships, and involvement in campus activities. Once prepared to enter the job market, an individual should use a variety of resources to locate excellent jobs in good companies. Many of the best jobs will be in companies graduates have never heard of.

GETTING THE BEST EDUCATION

Depending on an individual's career goals, the required background for a career in marketing may be gained in high school, vocational school, technical school, community college, college, university, or over the Internet. Educational requirements were discussed throughout the book as part of the specific job descriptions, so this chapter will focus on where to obtain this needed education and training. Most of the careers discussed in this book require college and university degrees and, in some cases, graduate study. Probably the most useful source of educational information on programs nationwide is *The College Blue Book*. This five-volume set is particularly useful to those seeking highly specialized programs. The volume entitled *Occupational Education* includes a listing of available programs of study in technical schools and community colleges, organized alphabetically by state or by subject area. Another volume, *Degrees Offered by College and Subject*, includes degree programs offered by two-year colleges, four-year colleges, and universities. Other volumes offer narrative descriptions of schools, costs, accreditation, enrollment figures, scholarships, fellowships, grants, loans, and a lot of other information.

The College Blue Book is found in the reference section of the library along with many other educational resources. Also available in most college and university libraries is a variety of college catalogs enabling one to compare curricula of different schools offering the degree or program of interest. Education is an important and expensive undertaking. A person should shop for it the way he or she would for any other important, expensive item. Gaining information from counselors, teachers, local colleges and universities, people working in the field, and potential employers is very advisable before selecting an educational program.

One important consideration when choosing a program is whether it has national accreditation. National bodies that accredit these schools are the American Association of Collegiate Schools of Business, the Association of Independent Colleges and Schools, the National Association of Trade and Technical Schools, and the National Home Study Council.

GAINING THE NECESSARY EXPERIENCE

As stressed throughout the book, experience is required for many of the more desirable marketing careers. This experience can be gained through internships and cooperative programs, part-time jobs, and involvement in campus activities.

Internships and Cooperative Programs

Traditional internships are usually three-month summer positions, while cooperative programs (co-ops) last a college quarter, semester, or longer. Internships are sometimes coordinated through an interested faculty member and a company manager, and the intern is not always paid. Co-ops, on the other hand, are part of an ongoing college program for which students receive both credits and pay. These distinctions aren't as clear anymore since companies want interns for longer periods, and they frequently offer paid internships. Many organizations hire their brightest interns and co-op students. As mentioned earlier, many professional associations offer information on internships available with member companies. Student membership in a number of professional associations is available at a reduced cost and is worth investigating.

Internships are advertised on college campuses through placement offices, on billboards, through faculty members, campus newspapers, and in books such as *Peterson's Internships 2000*. Online sources of internships can be found at websites such as InternshipPrograms.com.

Part-Time Jobs

Apart from intern and co-op programs, many students find part-time jobs on their own that offer both pay and experience. Most part-time jobs available to students are in sales. Though these jobs often pay minimum wage and are sometimes hard work, this work experience is very important to prospective employers. For one thing, the area of sales is vital to marketing—most activities in marketing are done to maximize sales and profits. Second, employers of part-time students can give important recommendations for full-time jobs. Prospective employers like to hear that an individual is reliable, works well with customers and coworkers, and has assumed an assistant manager role on occasion.

Many on-campus jobs can be obtained through student financial aid and job placement services. Located throughout every college campus are job boards and student publications advertising openings. Graduate assistantships are available to qualified students. Any opportunity for work experience prior to graduation should be considered because of the strength it lends to the job search for that first, very important, full-time job.

Involvement in Campus Activities

An option to all students is involvement in campus activities and organizations. By joining student business associations and taking a role in student government, students can develop the interpersonal skills needed in most marketing professions. Leadership experience in campus organizations is desirable to corporations. Though grade point average and work experience are very important, they do not always reveal the potential for leadership. Campus leaders rather than scholars are often hired for jobs in many business fields. The very charisma that helps students gain elective offices also scores high marks in job interviews. Participation in organized sports by both men and women also increases the strength of their resumes because learning how to be a good team player is an important lesson. Team playing, along with the acceptance that the coach may not always be right but is never wrong, has probably influenced promotion in corporations as much as academic preparation.

FINDING A GOOD JOB

Competition is always keen for good jobs, so graduates should develop job-finding skills as a necessary part of their education. The first full-time job out of college is particularly important because it sometimes sets the direction for an individual's entire career. The first step in the job search is to decide what attributes the individual wants in the job and how the job fits into overall career objectives.

Defining Career Objectives

Since all individuals do not define a good job in the same way, it is important for each job seeker to define what he or she wants in a job before beginning the search. For example, to an entry-level employee, a good job may be one offering growth through a formal company training program or company-financed continuing education; to an individual with a disability or to a parent with young children, a good job may be one that can be done in the home; to a student, a good job may be part-time or have flexible working hours; to a partner in a dual-career marriage, a good job may be one available locally; to an ambitious woman, a good job may be one in a company employing women managers in key positions. It is very important, however, for job seekers to have their individual requirements and career goals clearly in mind prior to launching the job search.

LOCATING JOBS

The task of finding a good job is twofold in that seekers must identify both companies with existing openings and companies for which they would like to work. The fact that a company does not have an advertised opening does not mean that the company would not create an opening for an outstanding applicant. This makes the job search more complicated, but it also offers the seeker considerably more opportunities. Students should build a network of family, friends, and associates who can refer them to others who might be able to help with their careers.

Many maintain that the way to find excellent jobs is through direct contact with the person who has the authority to hire. One of the best and most widely used books on the subject of job finding is *What Color Is Your Parachute?*, written by Richard Nelson Bolles. Although this book is not specifically for those seeking marketing careers, the strategies for conducting the job search are universal. This book helps the job seeker organize his or her time and energy and avoid tactics that rarely, if ever, pay off.

Various avenues for locating job opportunities include college placement offices, published job openings, recruiting firms, professional association placement services, job fairs or career days, and online recruitment services. These are discussed below.

College placement offices. Prospective college graduates should take advantage of the on-campus interviews arranged by the college placement office. Surveys of companies indicate that a large percentage of their new college hires come from these interviews. They provide an opportunity for a first contact with major company representatives while still on campus. Since these companies are recruiting for current job openings and are willing to hire beginners, young job seekers should definitely take advantage of these opportunities. It is best to sign up early because the company representatives have time for only a limited number of interviews. To prepare for these interviews, individuals should review the information on file in the college placement office. This information, provided by the interviewing companies, often includes annual reports and recruitment materials from which students can glean facts about a particular company and the career opportunities it offers.

Published job openings. A number of sources of listed job openings in business and marketing include *Peterson's Job Opportunities for Business and Liberal Arts Graduates*, *Career Employment Opportunities Directory*, and *Career Visions*. These books can usually be found in the career planning and placement office of most colleges and universities. They contain a tremendous amount of information, including listings of career opportunities, locations of employment, special training programs available with the companies, benefits, employer profiles, and addresses to write for further information. *Peterson's* also contains information on the job market as well as numerous job-seeking hints.

Professional journals provide another source of published job openings. Many journals devote a section near the end to advertising job openings. *The Wall Street Journal*, *New York Times*, and other big-city and local newspapers advertise openings, but responding to newspaper advertisements is rarely the way to obtain good jobs.

Recruiting firms. Some job opportunities are listed with recruiting firms. These firms provide needed services to both organizations and applicants. Although it is unusual for a beginner to find a highly desirable job through a recruiting firm, and often a sizable chunk of the first month's salary must be paid, these firms do offer some entry-level jobs that enable beginners to get much-needed experience. When demand is strong, many organizations seeking employees assume the charges for the service.

Professional association placement services. Many professional associations have placement services, including the following:

- National Association of Colleges and Employers, Bethlehem, PA

- Public Relations Society of America, New York, NY

- Society of Research Administrators, Chicago, IL

- Women in Communications, Inc., Arlington, VA

Even trade associations without placement services may provide directories of their members for free or at a minimal cost. Trade associations can often recommend or supply additional sources of information. Numerous professional associations and their addresses are listed throughout this book.

Job fairs or career days. College recruitment conferences are held in large cities around the country. These career conferences enable new graduates to meet employers who do not normally recruit on their campuses. Many schools and communities sponsor job fairs in which company representatives talk about opportunities within their firms. In addition, many offer seminars in job-seeking skills.

Online recruitment services. Online recruitment services are gaining in popularity numbering in the thousands. They make both job seekers and companies more accessible and are a very efficient way of exchanging information and asking and answering questions. Numerous websites offer thousands of job opportunities. In January 1999, 45 percent of Fortune Global 500 companies were actively recruiting over the Internet.[1] The big job boards provide listings of a variety of jobs in all areas where job seekers can uncover many possibilities after surfing for a few hours. In addition, candidates can assess their skills, build resumes, research companies, and take part in chat rooms or online classes. Free-agent sites provide a way for freelancers to connect with employers seeking candidates for short-term projects. Auction sites enable applicants to bid for projects or jobs. Niche sites, designed for specialized jobs and skills, are gaining in popularity. For positions in public relations, marketing, and advertising, PRandMarketingJobs.com sends a weekly E-letter with employment news and classified advertising.

Results of a survey published in the May 2000 issue of *Yahoo! Internet Life* pinpoint some of the best online job sites in different categories. They are mentioned below.

Best overall: monster.com

Best high-tech jobs: computerjobs.com

Best freelance jobs: guru.com

Best data on potential employers: vault.com

Best salary information: jobstar.org/tools/salary

Best resume tools and tips: eresumes.com

Best job-hunting tutorial: rileyguide.com

Best newspaper listings: careerpath.com

Best site for internships: review.com

Best metasearches: hoovers.com

Best relocation resource: homefair.com

Source: Alan Cohen, "We've Tested and Assessed, and Now—the Envelopes, Please," *Yahoo! Internet Life*, May 2000, pp. 111–112.

GAINING COMPANY INFORMATION

It is very important for an individual to have knowledge about the specific companies in which he or she will be interviewing.

Published information. Industry information is extremely valuable to the job seeker. Numerous sources of industry information are available. The current *U.S. Industrial Outlook* analyzes two hundred industries with projections into the future. It is published by the Bureau of Industrial Economics of the U.S.

Department of Commerce and can be found in the government documents section of the library. *Standard & Poor's Industry Surveys* include current and basic analyses for the major domestic industries. The current analysis includes latest industry developments; industry, market, and company statistics; and appraisals of investment outlook. The basic analysis includes prospects for the particular industry, an analysis of trends and problems; spotlights on major segments of the industry; growth in sales and earnings of leading companies in the industry; and other information over a ten-year span. Another excellent source of up-to-date industry information is *The Value Line Investment Survey*.

Many sources focus on specific companies. The *Dun & Bradstreet Directories*, *Moody's Manuals*, and *Thomas's Register* all provide specific company information, such as the address and phone number of the company, what the business produces, its annual sales, and the names of officers and directors. If an individual is interested in the backgrounds of those who make it to the top in a particular company, *Standard & Poor's Register of Corporations, Directors, and Executives* and *Dun & Bradstreet's Reference Book of Corporate Managements* both provide this type of information. These resources are found in public and college libraries in the reference section. Annual and quarterly corporate reports are usually housed in the college career placement offices.

The following list of directories includes listings for specific areas in marketing:

Standard Directory of Advertising Agencies

Consultants and Consulting Organizations Directory

Dun's Consultant's Directory

Franchise Annual

The Sourcebook of Franchise Opportunities

Bradford's Directory of Marketing Research Agencies and Management Consultants in the United States and the World

The Green Book: International Directory of Marketing Research Houses and Services

O'Dwyer's Directory of Public Relations Firms

Online information. As mentioned, the site rated best for company information is vault.com, which includes information from employee surveys across a range of industries. Such inside information as the interview process and the dress code is covered along with company business and relevant market information. Many companies have their own websites with much valuable information.

Information on companies can be used by the job seeker to prepare a list of employers to contact, to eliminate companies with low growth potential, to identify a job target for the resume, and to compile a list of intelligent questions that will impress any interviewer.

Other information. Another way to gain information about what is happening in companies in the marketing field is by reading professional journals. Along with advertised openings, these journals provide a wealth of information to help the job seeker ask timely and well-informed questions during the interview and to make a final decision on what company would be the best employer.

THE RESUME

The first contact that most individuals have with a company is the resume. It has to be good or a job applicant may never gain an interview. It's often said that you never have a second chance to make a good first impression. Every statement should show how an applicant is qualified for the position he or she seeks. As a reflection of one's skill in written communication, it is a perfect way to bias the interviewer on an applicant's behalf before he or she even walks through the door. A resume is basically a sales device. It should do three things. First, it should emphasize the most positive features in an individual's background, such as maintaining an A average in college. Second, it should stress work experience and positive contributions to former employers. Third, it should describe positive personal attributes and abilities. Individuals themselves write the best resumes rather than professional resume-preparation services. Only individuals can present themselves in their best light and sound truthful doing it. It is wise, however, to get some editorial help from a career counselor or other skilled individual since the resume should make the best possible impression.

Resume Basics

The following are some basic hints for writing a good resume:

1. People usually skim resumes. Too many numbers, too much verbiage, poor spacing, and unclear headings all make a resume difficult to skim. Strongest positive points should be made first.

2. No matter how terrific a person is or how much experience he or she has had, a resume for a new college graduate should not exceed two pages. Job-seekers should only use more pages if their experience is sufficient to qualify them for a management position and/or after excluding all nonessential information, such as information on hobbies. One should stick to the facts and save philosophy for the interview, if asked about it. Unnecessary words such as "I," "he," or "she" should be eliminated. Resumes are usually written in phrases—not complete sentences.

3. Action words such as "coordinated," "supervised," and "developed" should be used. A resume should be oriented toward results and accomplishments rather than duties. The tone should be as positive as the content.

4. The resume should be free of spelling or grammatical errors and neatly typed or printed on white or ivory rag paper. No fancy binders should be used.

5. Salaries, reasons for termination, references, supervisors' names, politics, religion, race, ethnic background, sex, height, weight, and pictures should be excluded.

6. An individually typed cover letter should be used each time a resume is sent to a prospective employer. The letter should be addressed to a specific person whenever possible. In it, applicants introduce themselves, explain the reason for writing, describe potential contributions to the company, and request an interview. A job target should be identified in the cover letter if a target resume is not used. Copies of all letters sent should be kept in one file folder; responses requiring action by the applicant should be kept in a second; and rejection letters should be kept in a third.

With the above basics clearly in mind, the applicant should write a resume that is a summary of his or her skills, education, work experience, interests, career goals, and any other information that qualifies that individual for the position sought.

Resume Formats

Different formats may be used in developing a resume. The type of format used depends on the background of the individual.

Chronological resumes. A commonly used format is a chronological arrangement of educational and work experiences, each listed separately with the most recent experience first. If an applicant is seeking a job that is a natural progression from former jobs and has a good work history with growth and development, this is a good format to use. However, if an applicant's former work history consists of part-time jobs while in college, there is a better format—the functional arrangement.

Functional resumes. A resume organized around functional or topical headings stresses competencies. Such headings as "Research" and "Marketing" enable an individual to include coursework, special projects, and work experience. These headings are geared to the type of position the applicant is seeking. Actual work experience is included at the bottom of the resume. Both functional and chronological resumes can be used for broad career objectives.

Targeted resumes. A type of resume used widely today is the targeted resume. Jobs have become more specific and highly defined than they used to be. Beginners who are aware of the job market will have developed some special areas of expertise in order to make them viable applicants for some of the best positions. The job target is clearly stated along with specific areas of expertise related to the applicant's ability to do the job.

Which resume format is best is a function of the applicant's experience and career objectives. A good resume increases the likelihood that an individual will be contacted for an interview. This contact is often by phone, so the job seeker should keep a pad and pen beside the phone to record any information from such calls. The more organized and in control an applicant appears, the more impressed prospective employers will be.

Before putting a resume online, one should be aware of some privacy pitfalls and some things that can be done about them. In a *Fortune* article, some useful suggestions are made by author Jerry Useem.[2] If a person wants to change jobs, there is a chance that his boss may end up receiving or coming across his resume. It's a good idea to date online resumes in case your boss comes across an old copy and erroneously thinks that you want to change jobs. You can also include a legend that forbids headhunters from transmitting it without your permission. Before posting your resume to an online site, ask the administrators who has access to the database and whether resumes are traded or sold to other databases. If currently employed, you can list qualifications but withhold your name and have inquiries go to an anonymous E-mail account. An alternative to posting your resume online is to register with a job agent service on sites like Nation.com and CareerBuilder.com and they will notify you of job openings. Some students use multimedia technology to create "cyber-portfolios" that contain personalized voice and photo greetings, links to previous employer Web pages, and displays of college projects and special interest items.[3]

Excellent books for information on resume writing include *Resumes for College Students and Recent Graduates*, *Resumes for Advertising Careers*, and *Resumes for Sales and Marketing Careers*, published by VGM Career Books, 4255 W. Touhy Avenue, Lincolnwood, IL 60712.

PREPARING FOR THE INTERVIEW

Preparing for a job interview involves a lot more than putting on clothes. An earlier section described sources of information on specific companies. It is sometimes possible for an individual to obtain a schedule of his or her visit to the company in advance, including the names and titles of the interviewers. If any are senior managers, their backgrounds could be researched in an industry *Who's Who* or another source, and some aspect of this background could be casually referred to during the interview. A job candidate could also request a sample copy of any standard employee newsletter, relevant company publication, or an annual company stockholder report.

Since the applicant has some time during the interview process to ask questions, it is best to have developed a list of critical questions, some based on the preinterview research. Examples of such questions include the following: What type of performance appraisal system is used? How is the company's career development system set up, and what are some common career paths within the company? How are new workers trained and developed? How long has the prospective supervisor held that position? What is the management style of the company? In what direction is future growth anticipated? In short, any information that the applicant has been unable to gain in advance that might heavily affect his or her career development should be learned in the interview, if possible.

Conservative dress—without looking uniformed—is usually safe attire for a job interview. Women might wear a simply tailored suit, a neat hairdo, plain jewelry, and moderate makeup and perfume. Men might wear a conservative suit, shirt, and tie. Polished shoes, trimmed and styled hair, and clean fingernails are also all important.

Posture is significant, as are all types of body language. A firm handshake, good eye contact, poise, ease, and manners all contribute to a positive interview. The novice job applicant might even improve his or her overall performance at a job interview by practicing beforehand in front of a mirror.

A portfolio of college experiences might be useful to show to a prospective employer at the job interview. This portfolio can include best class papers; descriptions of projects completed for class, internships, or jobs; and fliers from events a student participated in or helped organize such as seminars or club fund-raising events. Anything related to the job sought should be put in the portfolio.

THE INTERVIEW

Each corporation has a unique corporate culture. An applicant's ability to fit into this culture is often the key to being hired. Sizing up the corporate culture is something an applicant can do by walking into a lobby. Is there elaborate security or a club-like atmosphere? Is the coffee served in fine china or plastic cups? Do the executives sometimes pick up their own phones? Are only degrees and certificates displayed in the offices, or family photos as well? The applicant's ability to discern the degree of formality or informality and modify interview behaviors accordingly might make the difference between a job offer or disappointment. The fact is that managers are not only looking for levels of experience but for types of individuals who would fit comfortably into the organization. In other words, chemistry between candidate and interviewer is critical. Both need to determine whether or not they would like to work together daily. This is a highly subjective factor.

The applicants most likely to be hired are effective communicators both on professional and personal levels. Marketing graduates have an edge because most of them know how to sell things—including themselves. They are warm, outgoing, enthusiastic, and self-confident. Both the applicant and interviewer are under stress. The more relaxed both manage to be during the interview, the better the interview will be and the more information will be exchanged. The interviewer is looking at both substance, which is basically a person's past performance, and style, which includes communication skills, poise, self-confidence, and motivation. Broad questions such as "How would you describe yourself?" and "How can you contribute to our organization?" reveal the applicant's values and personality and how the applicant organizes his or her thoughts. How a person fields questions also shows performance under pressure, quickness, energy, and sense of humor.

In general, employers regard specific skills and experience as more important qualifications than educational background. Such skills as written and verbal communication, related work experience, and knowledge of the functions of the company are very important. This is not to say that grade point average and coursework are not scrutinized also. The point is that most employers care more about what you can do for their company than what you have learned in college, so in both the resume and the interview job seekers should focus on the skills they possess and the value of these skills to the company.

Often a member of the human resources department conducts a preliminary interview. This interview determines whether or not a candidate will fit into the corporate culture. If this interview goes well for the candidate, the manager of the department in which the applicant would work conducts a second interview. An applicant should ask questions as the interview progresses or, if the interviewer shows a high need for structure, should wait until asked if there are any questions. The applicant's questions should emphasize professional growth and work-related activities. Such topics as salary and benefits should be discussed after the job is offered. Some bargaining may then occur, particularly if the applicant has another offer in hand.

Ironically, most applicants forget to ask for the job. An applicant should both ask for the job and thank the interviewer. Some indication of when the applicant will hear from the company should be given. The interest that an interviewer shows in an applicant does not mean that a job will be offered. It is standard operating procedure; the interviewer is building goodwill and keeping the applicant interested. Applicants should go on as many interviews as possible and carefully compare companies and offers, no matter how well a first interview goes or how certain an applicant is that a job will be offered. Additional offers both provide an individual with choices and give some leverage to the applicant who can then bargain for salary and benefits.

A person is his or her own best resource. By using good judgment in choosing and planning a career, by gaining information from a variety of sources, by relying on well-formulated questions as well as intuition in accepting a job, an individual can increase chances of success in a marketing career.

1. Useem, Jerry. "For Sale Online: You." *Fortune*, July 5, 1999, 76.
2. Useem, Jerry. "Read This Before You Put a Resume Online." *Fortune*, May 24, 1999, 290–292.
3. Siegmann, Bob. "Cyber-Portfolios: A New Tool for Job Seekers." *T.H.E. Journal*, February 1998, 58–59.

JOB INDEX